DID JESUS HAVE A GIRLFRIEND?

DID JESUS HAVE A GIRLFRIEND?

And Other Tricky Questions about Jesus

JOHN HONNER

A GUIDE FOR TEACHERS, CATECHISTS, AND PARENTS

Paulist Press
New York / Mahwah, NJ

Cover image courtesy of St Edmund's College, Canberra, Australia.
Cover and book design by Lynn Else

Library of Congress Cataloging-in-Publication Data
Names: Honner, John, author.
Title: Did Jesus have a girlfriend? : and other tricky questions about Jesus : a guide for teachers, catechists, and parents / John Honner.
Description: New York ; Mahwah, New Jersey : Paulist Press, [2022] | Summary: "In this sequel to Does God Like Being God? this book explores questions about Jesus: who he was, what he did, and his importance to Christians"—Provided by publisher.
Identifiers: LCCN 2021052567 (print) | LCCN 2021052568 (ebook) | ISBN 9780809155958 (paperback) | ISBN 9781587689970 (ebook)
Subjects: LCSH: Jesus Christ—Person and offices—Miscellanea. | Catholic Church—Doctrines—Miscellanea.
Classification: LCC BT203 .H655 2022 (print) | LCC BT203 (ebook) | DDC 232—dc23/eng/20211130
LC record available at https://lccn.loc.gov/2021052567
LC ebook record available at https://lccn.loc.gov/2021052568

ISBN 978-0-8091-5595-8 (paperback)
ISBN 978-1-58768-997-0 (e-book)

Published by Paulist Press
997 Macarthur Boulevard
Mahwah, New Jersey 07430
www.paulistpress.com

Printed and bound in the
United States of America

In memory of Michael John Bowden (1947–2020)
and in acknowledgment of my great indebtedness to my beloved friends

CONTENTS

CONTENTS

ACKNOWLEDGMENTS

I very much want to acknowledge all my special friends—you know who you are—for teaching me about love. I thank particularly my extraordinary wife, Colleen, my extended family, and all those good people in the Christian communities and institutions that I have lived and labored among for your love and encouragement.

Despite the difficulties of working during the COVID epidemic, the staff at Paulist Press have remained attentive and upbeat. Paul McMahon has steered this somewhat eccentric ship through to publication with sensitive editing and several marked improvements. Thank you.

This work is dedicated to the memory of Michael Bowden: husband, lover, father, would-be priest, champion of Australian football, teacher, student, prophet, strong and tender friend to many, especially the *Arrernte* people of central Australia. Michael met Jesus Christ in every face, in every culture, in every element of life. He died on Holy Saturday in 2020, between crucifixion and resurrection. We had talked a great deal about what this book might be. As the work was coming to completion, however, he was in the final stages of motor neurone disease and no longer able to speak. When I asked him if any of his six wonderful children had ever posed tricky questions about Jesus to him or to his wife and soul mate Jude, he wrote back, "No tricky questions. We just lived lives full of love and they learnt to love and live generously." Where there is Love, there is Jesus.

INTRODUCTION

HIGH FIVE JESUS

St. Edmund's College is a high school in Canberra, the capital city of Australia, that has a small well-worn statue of Jesus at a turning point in the main corridor of the central building. It is a memorial to a boy who, long ago, died too young. The statue isn't in a niche in the wall, nor is it high up on a plinth. It's not in a chapel. It stands on the floor, on the same level as the students who walk past it many times each day. It's not a particularly beautiful statue, but that seems to be of no concern to the students. Over the years, they have taken to shaking the statue's outstretched hand and, more recently, giving Jesus a high five. All the paint and glazing have now been stripped away, revealing worn fingers, calloused with dark gravel. The statue is known among the students as High Five Jesus.

The statue is an image of a Jesus whom students can begin to relate to because the statue is at their level. It is among them. Jesus shares *their* sign of friendship. He cares about their living and their dying. It reminds us that *our relationship with* Jesus is more fundamental than *our doctrine about* Jesus. Pope Francis, in an exhortation to young people, makes this clear:

> In some places, it happens that young people are helped to have a powerful experience of God, an encounter with Jesus that touched their hearts. But the only follow-up to this is a series of "formation" meetings featuring talks about doctrinal and moral issues, the evils of today's world, the Church, her social doctrine, chastity, marriage, birth control and so on. As a result, many young people get bored, they lose the fire of their encounter with Christ and the joy of following him; many give up and others become downcast or negative. Rather than being too concerned with communicating a great deal of doctrine, let us first try to awaken and consolidate the great experiences that sustain the Christian life.[1]

---

1. Pope Francis, *Christus Vivit* (March 25, 2019), §212.

Worrying over the doctrinal issues stirred up by the questions young people ask about Jesus, I started to have doubts about this project. Young people can hold controversial views. They can ask challenging questions. How can Church teaching or my dry theological contributions help? Could I afford to appear irreverent? I could sense trouble ahead. At the same time as these questions were bothering me, I happened to be reading Kate Hennessy's sometimes irreverent and controversial biography of her grandmother, Dorothy Day. Kate explained how, in her later years, Dorothy was no longer silent "on the disorderly life she led before her conversion," and spoke often and easily of "the joy and seeking and questioning." Dorothy had said, "We're born to ask questions....It's a tragedy to go through life not asking....God wants us to ask."[2]

That's the nature of youth: some disorder, much joy, and a lot of seeking and questioning. Every young person will ask their unique questions in a different context. The attention and love of parents and teachers are the most important elements of a response for a young person. When young people seek answers, we should reverence their questions because, as Francis put it, "Each young person's heart should thus be considered 'holy ground,' a bearer of seeds of divine life, before which we must 'take off our shoes' in order to draw near and enter more deeply into the Mystery."[3]

Young people are also helped when the Church is authentic and the answers to their questions about Christian faith are plausible and informed.[4] Hence, this book is intended to assist parents, teachers, and catechists—and maybe preachers too—in shaping reasonable and informed replies to young people's questions. It offers foundations, frameworks, and suggestions that you can use in your own way and with your own expertise, depending on each young person's situation.

This work is a sequel to *Does God Like Being God? And Other Tricky Questions about God.*[5] I will not repeat here material from the introductory chapters of that book, except to note that they explained the simplicity of theological method, the importance of the Bible, the reasonableness of faith, and the conditions for the development of Church teaching. Some of those tricky questions about God, especially the ones on suffering, noted the need for a follow-up book about how God might come among us—a book about Jesus. This is it!

---

2. Kate Hennessy, *Dorothy Day: The World Will Be Saved by Beauty* (New York: Scribner, 2017), 51.

3. Pope Francis, *Christus Vivit*, §67.

4. See, e.g., the research reported in Richard Rymarz, *Creating an Authentic Catholic School* (Montréal: Novalis, 2016).

5. John Honner, *Does God Like Being God? And Other Tricky Questions about God* (Mahwah, NJ: Paulist Press, 2019).

These reflections arose in the same circumstances as the earlier book. They are the harvest of many years of teaching theology and supervising graduate courses for religious education coordinators and school leaders in Catholic education. Participants liked the way I explained theology and explored the difficult questions that students ask. I thank them for passing these questions on to me! They asked why nobody had given these answers before, and if I could put these ideas in a book.

We begin by engaging the young person in their unique history and context. We must always respond to the person asking the question before we go about answering the question. Francis does this admirably in his replies to the questions that children sent him from all around the world. For example, an eight-year-old girl called Natasha from Kenya asked him how Jesus walked on water. She attached a drawing of Jesus walking on water with lots of fish swimming below. Francis, noting the fish in her drawing and entering into her imagination, replied,

Dear Natasha,

You have to imagine Jesus walking naturally, normally. He did not fly over the water or turn somersaults while swimming. He walked as you walk! He walked, one foot after the other, as if the water were land. He walked on the water's surface as he saw the fish under his feet frolicking or racing around.

Jesus is God, and so he can do anything! He can walk safely on water. God cannot sink, you know![6]

This may be the right answer for an eight-year-old child. It worked for me when Mother Anthony, IBVM, brought a large bowl of water into my school class at Kirribilli when I was six or seven. She shook the bowl so that waves went back and forth. "Water be still!" she commanded. Nothing happened. "But Jesus," she said, "commanded the sea to be still, and it was." Then and there I learned that Jesus was very special.

A sixteen-year-old person, however, will rarely be satisfied by these kinds of explanations. They want plausible and reasonable answers. Perhaps the real point of Jesus walking on water is not that he stilled the waves like a magician, *but that he cared for his friends when they were in trouble, and he took away their deepest fears.* Perhaps he also walked on water—see chapter 8 to find out more.

---

6. Pope Francis, in conversation with Antonio Spadaro, *Dear Pope Francis: The Pope Answers Letters from Children around the World* (Chicago: Loyola Press, 2016), 9.

In this book, in trying to give reasonable answers to questions about our faith, I use a systematic theological method that entails nine steps:

1. What is the concern of the questioner?
2. What light does Scripture shine on the question?
3. What light does the tradition of the Church shine on the question?
4. What is the current teaching of the Church regarding the question?
5. What are the needs and concerns of the people in the community of faith?
6. What can we discern of the movement of the Holy Spirit in the Church?
7. Are there any relevant findings in secular sciences that we should consider?
8. What new understandings emerge from all these reflections?
9. How does the community of faith respond to our findings?

These are basic steps for doing theology. Occasionally, putting on my physicist's hat and engaging questions young people ask about the miracles in Jesus's life, there are some paragraphs and postscripts on relevant scientific information.

Readers may start wherever they wish in this book. We begin with the tricky questions that young people ask and that, sometimes, theologians have not considered. Those interested in the background questions may find it helpful to start near the end, with Part Two, "Advanced Questions." It is intended to help parents and teachers grow further into an adult faith and be even more capable of responding to young people's questions. There is a chapter on the reliability of the Gospels, a chapter on how to travel with the Gospels, a chapter on faith and delusion, and a chapter on the significance of what the Creeds and *Catechism* say about Jesus. Finally, the Conclusion to the book, "Where to from here?," suggests, among other things, going beyond indoctrination to *exdoctrination.*

While there is a risk that theological critiques can weaken the personal faith in Jesus we developed as children, holy theologians can provide good counsel. The American Lutheran theologian Marcus Borg, for example, realized that his faith in Jesus was gradually being eroded by his scholarly approach to the Gospels. His change of heart produced a book with the marvelous title *Meeting Jesus Again for the First Time: The Historical Jesus and the Heart of Contemporary Faith.* He writes, "For many Christians...there came a time when their childhood image of Jesus no longer made a great deal of sense. And for many of them, no persuasive alternative has replaced it....For them, meeting Jesus again will be—as it has been for me—like meeting him for the first time. It will involve a new image of Jesus."[7] My aim is to help people, young and old, develop not only a new image of Jesus but also a new closeness to Jesus, as if meeting Jesus again for the first time. I am guided by young people's questions, the loving wisdom of Jesus's followers and friends, and the scholarship of theologians.

In the beginning there were only four widely accepted books about Jesus, namely the Gospels of Matthew, Mark, Luke, and John. Now there are millions. I have been reading books about Jesus for more than fifty years.[8] Where to start? I happened to have on my desk three very different studies of Jesus, two of them comprehensive in their own way, produced by distinguished scholars who shared the same desire to follow the living Jesus more closely. These studies had arrived almost by coincidence: one came as part of a teaching project, one came from a relative who found it too hard to read, and one came as a Christmas present. Each offered its own insights and images of Jesus. First, there is Benedict XVI's three volume study of *Jesus of Nazareth*,[9] which he writes as Joseph Ratzinger rather than as pope, and which moves from a detailed survey of tradition and scholarship to a living faith in Jesus. Second, there is Marcus Borg's *Meeting Jesus Again for the First Time*, mentioned above, which tells the story of finding a living Jesus. And, finally, there is José Pagola's *Jesus: An Historical Approximation*,[10] written by a believer, but using historical rigor to describe Jesus's person and message for his followers today. They have proven to be perfect guides.

Many other saints, scholars, women, men, poets, and artists have helped shape my answers to the tricky questions that young people ask about Jesus.[11] Because this book is for a general readership, technical words and scholarly footnotes will be kept to a minimum. As for most of us, my best teachers in Christ are those loving ones who imitate Jesus in their profound humanity and self-giving, in their hope and joy, and in their falling into the arms of God.

---

7. Marcus J. Borg, *Meeting Jesus Again for the First Time: The Historical Jesus and the Heart of Contemporary Faith* (New York: HarperCollins, 1995), 1.

8. In 1963, I won Giuseppe Ricciotti's *Life of Christ* for coming first in religious knowledge in my high school! The book that had the greatest impact on me, however, was Eduard Schweizer's *Jesus*, from 1971. The statue became a person!

9. Joseph Ratzinger, *Jesus of Nazareth: The Infancy Narratives* (2012); *Jesus of Nazareth: From the Baptism in the Jordan to the Transfiguration* (2007); *Jesus of Nazareth: From the Entrance into Jerusalem to the Resurrection* (2011). The three-volume set is now available from Ignatius Press.

10. José Pagola, *Jesus: An Historical Approximation*, rev. ed. (Miami: Convivium, 2015).

11. I acknowledge, especially, Joan E. Taylor and Joan Wright Howie for their major contributions to chap. 2.

Part One

QUESTIONS ABOUT JESUS

1

DID JESUS REALLY EXIST?

Yes, Jesus really did exist! Jesus was just as real as other historical figures like Buddha or Cleopatra. He was not a made-up fictional character like Superwoman or Harry Potter. There actually was someone called Jesus of Nazareth. He lived two thousand years ago, and he was a real human being.

How can we be so confident? There are three sets of data that fit together. First, there is the evidence from the Gospels. The Gospel of Luke stresses that Jesus lived in a particular place at a particular time. In the opening chapters, we find many historical details:

> "In the days of King Herod of Judea, there was a priest named Zechariah, who belonged to the priestly order of Abijah" (Luke 1:5).

> "In those days a decree went out from Emperor Augustus that all the world should be registered. This was the first registration and was taken while Quirinius was governor of Syria" (Luke 2:1–2).

> "In the fifteenth year of the reign of Emperor Tiberius, when Pontius Pilate was governor of Judea, and Herod was ruler of Galilee, and his brother Philip ruler of the region of Ituraea and Trachonitis, and Lysanias ruler of Abilene, during the high priesthood of Annas and Caiaphas" (Luke 3:1–2).

Second, although they had no reason to promote Christianity, there are Roman and Jewish writers who mention Jesus. Josephus, writing toward the end of the first century, mentions "Jesus, a wise man...a doer of wonderful works, a teacher of those who receive the truth with pleasure." The Roman historian Tacitus, no friend of Christians, mentions "Christ, who, during the reign of Tiberius, had been executed by the procurator Pontius Pilate." A contemporary historian, Suetonius, writes of a certain "Chresus," whose followers were expelled from Rome by the emperor Claudius.[1]

It is true that there are no concrete historical signs of Jesus having ever lived. There are no coins, no statues, no inscriptions on a tomb, but there are no historical signs of most people from those times. There is, however, increasing archaeological evidence in support of the Gospel stories. In 1962, a damaged inscription of "[Pont]ius Pilate" on a limestone block was discovered in Caesarea. In 1968, the first-century tomb of a crucified man was discovered with nails through his feet—not that this was Jesus. In 1986, the remains of a first-century sailing boat were found in the Sea of Galilee. The boat carried oars and a mast, with room for thirteen people. And in 1990, the tomb of a son of a Caiaphas dating back to the time of Jesus was found in Jerusalem.[2]

Some might argue that the claims made for Jesus are too outrageous for him to have been real. How could he walk on water, for example, or cast the Gadarene swine into the sea when the sea of Galilee is five miles from Gadara? This argument is irrelevant, here, because it questions *what Jesus is said to have done* more than *whether he really existed*. There were never any doubts in the ancient world about whether Jesus existed, even though there were arguments about whether Jesus was the Messiah.

This brings us to the third and final reason for believing that Jesus really existed. Would Jesus's followers—women, men, apostles, and disciples—have given their lives for a fictitious character? Would they have endured the persecution recorded in both the Roman histories and the Acts of the Apostles? Other would-be messiahs, revolutionaries, teachers, and healers around the time of Jesus had many followers—remember Barabbas—but these all faded away. Why then did Jesus's followers persevere? It is reasonable to conclude that Jesus was real. People do not give their lives for a fiction.

True, there is some debate about exactly where and when Jesus was born. Some say that he may have been born in Nazareth because only Matthew and Luke mention Bethlehem, but that is a long bow, and the Bethlehem story has a ring of truth about it. Astronomers have suggested that the bright star seen at Jesus's birth could only have been an overlapping of Venus and Jupiter, which occurred both seven and two years earlier than AD 1 (*Anno Domini*, the year of the Lord). These are speculations. Nonetheless, Jesus was very likely not born on Christmas day, because the first known references to December 25 as Jesus's birthday occur much later, in a Roman

---

1. For references to the detailed evidence, see J. G. D. Dunn, *Jesus Remembered* (Grand Rapids, MN: Eerdmans, 2003), 141–42. Claudius was emperor from AD 41 to 54.

2. See Pagola, *Jesus*, 487–91.

calendar of AD 336. The date was probably chosen to replace a pagan celebration that had been held at that time in the centuries before the Roman Empire adopted Christianity as its official religion in AD 323. Others argue that Jesus could not have been born in midwinter, because the presence of shepherds indicates that lambs had been recently born, and so Jesus must have been born in the northern spring. These speculations about the where and when of Jesus's birth count for little against the claim that Jesus actually was born, even if we do not know precisely where or when.

The much more important question is not whether Jesus was real, but what Jesus was like, whether Jesus was really both human and divine, and how we can get to know him today. So read on!

2

WHAT DID JESUS LOOK LIKE?
WHAT DID HE WEAR?

Most young people are concerned about body image and having the right clothes to wear. Unfortunately, looks and fashion seem to be of no concern to the Gospel writers. We know nothing about Jesus's physical appearance—whether he was tall or short, or striking or average. This may seem extraordinary, given that we know so much about where he journeyed, what he taught, and how he healed people. Yet, there was nothing remarkable about his appearance. His neighbors in Nazareth thought he was just another ordinary young man in the village (see, e.g., Luke 4:22). When he cured a man on the Sabbath in Jerusalem, and the authorities went looking for him, he had "disappeared in the crowd" (John 5:13). Perhaps we are not meant to know what he looked like. Maybe Jesus includes all and excludes none.

Nonetheless, we can say that Jesus probably looked like any other Jewish man: dark hair, dark eyes, olive skin. His hair was probably short rather than long, given that short hair was the fashion of his time. He could not have looked anything like the pale-skinned, blue-eyed, fair-haired images of Jesus in Western art, because such extraordinary features would most likely have been remarked on somewhere in the Gospels.

Joan Taylor argues from archaeological evidence and the earliest images of Jesus that he may have had shortish hair and a clipped beard.[1] She notes that the anti-Christian philosopher Celsus, writing a century after the death of Jesus, claimed to have gathered information from Jews and others to the effect that Jesus "wandered about most shamefully in the sight of all" and "obtained his means of livelihood in a disgraceful and importunate way." This suggests that Jesus probably looked

---

1. For a thorough study, see Joan E. Taylor, *What Did Jesus Look Like?* (London: Bloomsbury, 2018).

"scruffy."[2] Celsus was critical of Christianity, and his observations may be biased, but there may also be a grain of truth in them.

While we have no detailed description of Jesus's physical appearance in the Gospels, there are several reports of a radiant glory surrounding him. We read that while Jesus was praying, "the appearance of his face changed, and his clothes became dazzling white" (Luke 9:29). Or again, that "his face shone like the sun, and his clothes became dazzling white" (Matt 17:1–3). And that "we have seen his glory, the glory as of a father's only son, full of grace and truth" (John 1:14). Scholars tell us that, in the Hebrew tradition, the "dazzling white" meant something different from what it means in our own time. White, here, is not so much a color as a luminousness. Sometimes there was a great aura about Jesus.

For most of the time, though, it seems that Jesus looked very much like the people around him. Mary Magdalene, after the resurrection, thought he was a gardener. On the road to Emmaus as by the Sea of Galilee, his best friends did not recognize him. They recognized him more in his actions and his words than in his physical characteristics. The risen Jesus has a different look about him. We know him by his heart and his Spirit. He tells us we will meet him when we gather in his name, share consecrated bread and wine, visit the poor and the sick, the blind and the lame, the widow and the orphan, and the prisoner and the stranger.

* * *

We come, now, to our second question, "What did Jesus wear?" Like his contemporaries, Jesus would have possessed few clothes. They would have been homemade, using a linen fabric woven from a small loom. The clothing at the time consisted of a tunic like a long T-shirt, maybe with a girdle or belt. For men, the tunic went down to the knee; for women, it went down to the ankles. He possibly wore a loin cloth under the tunic. Over the tunic, he would have worn an undyed, woolen shawl with a fringe, which would have been fixed around his body and thrown over one shoulder (see Mark 6:56). He often wore sandals (see Matthew 3:11; Mark 1:7; Mark 6:9; John 1:27), but possibly also went barefoot.[3] On his journeys he probably carried a staff. Jesus surely would have worn the same things he told his disciples to wear: "He ordered them to take nothing for their journey except a staff; no bread, no bag, no money in their belts; but to wear sandals and not to put on two tunics" (Mark 6:8–9).

---

2. See Joan E. Taylor, "What Did Jesus Wear?," February 8, 2018, https://theconversation.com/what-did-jesus-wear-90783.

3. Pagola suggests that Jesus may also have gone barefoot, like a slave, and expected his disciples to do the same: hence the command to shake the dust off their feet, not their sandals (see Matt 10:14, Mark 6:11, and Luke 9:5).

His cousin John the Baptist was said to wear "clothing of camel's hair with a leather belt around his waist" (Matt 3:4). What was important about John the Baptist was not what he wore, but who he was, a prophet. We read in the Gospel of Matthew,

> Jesus began to speak to the crowds about John: "What did you go out into the wilderness to look at? A reed shaken by the wind? What then did you go out to see? Someone dressed in soft robes? Look, those who wear soft robes are in royal palaces. What then did you go out to see? A prophet? Yes, I tell you, and more than a prophet." (Matt 11:7–9)

There are claimed images of Jesus, like the Veil of Veronica and the Shroud of Turin, but these are more matters of devotion than of history. The Gospels are much more interested in his message than in his appearance, except perhaps during his passion and death. And part of Jesus's message is not to worry about appearances:

> I tell you, do not worry about your life, what you will eat or what you will drink, or about your body, what you will wear. Is not life more than food, and the body more than clothing?...Consider the lilies of the field, how they grow; they neither toil nor spin, yet I tell you, even Solomon in all his glory was not clothed like one of these. But if God so clothes the grass of the field, which is alive today and tomorrow is thrown into the oven, will he not much more clothe you—you of little faith? (Matt 6:25–30; see also Luke 12:22–31)

Nonetheless, clothes are a good thing. At one time, after he had brought peace to a wild, homeless, naked outcast, the man is seen "sitting at the feet of Jesus, clothed and in his right mind" (Luke 8:35).

The New Testament does tell us what to wear, but it is more than clothes. The Greek word *enkomboomai* occurs several times in the New Testament. It is usually translated as "clothe yourself with" or "put on," and we are variously told to *enkomboomai* ourselves with love; with the armor of light; with the armor of God; with the breastplate of righteousness; with power from on high; with the imperishable; with our dwelling from heaven; with a heart of compassion, kindness, humility, gentleness, and patience; with a new self; and, above all, with Christ, the Lord Jesus Christ.[4] We go clothed in Jesus's compassion and God's Spirit. We should give clothes to those

---

4. See Col 3:14–17; Rom 13:12; Eph 6:11, 14; 2 Cor 5:2; Luke 24:49; 1 Cor 15:54; Col 3:12; Eph 4:24; Gal 3:27; and Rom 13:14.

who have none, but not worry about the superficial differences between ourselves and our companions, for in Christ we are all equally brothers and sisters.[5]

Jesus may have been very short. You can get a young person's attention here with a dad joke. We know Jesus was very short because the Gospel of Luke tells us so. Remember Zacchaeus? He was the tax collector who climbed a tree. Luke tells us that he was trying to see who Jesus was, "but on account of the crowd he could not, because he was short in stature" (Luke 19:3). Who was short in stature? We all assume it was Zacchaeus, but the second "he" may refer to Jesus! This "he" was *mikros*, meaning very small. Joke or not, small is okay with Jesus. He had dinner with Zacchaeus later that day.

---

5. Many elements of this chapter, and particularly these final paragraphs, are indebted to Joan Wright Howie's "What Would Jesus Wear?" and the Habitat Uniting Church in Melbourne, Australia, June 4, 2013, https://www.habitatforspirituality .org.au/ministers-blog/what-would-jesus-wear.

3

WAS JESUS FUN TO BE WITH?

Fun seems to be an important word for young people. Church seems boring. Could Jesus possibly have been fun? If fun means good times, then the disciples had their moments. The sourpuss Pharisees, for example, complained about Jesus: "Why do you eat and drink with tax collectors and sinners?" They then attacked his disciples, saying, "John's disciples, like the disciples of the Pharisees, frequently fast and pray, but your disciples eat and drink" (Luke 5:30–33).

If fun means inspiration and adventure, then absolutely, Jesus was fun to be with. But *fun* is not a word we find in the Gospels. Instead, we find *joy*, a deeper kind of fun. At Jesus's birth, an angel announced news of great joy for all the people (see Luke 1:47; 2:9–10). Jesus tells his friends, "No one will take your joy from you" (John 16:22). Jesus wants us all to be happy. Jesus was not a killjoy. As José Pagola observes,

> There was another trait that Jesus wanted to encourage within his group: joy....They had no reason to fast or mourn. Living with him was a feast.... The meals were the best part. Jesus taught them to celebrate the recovery of so many lost people with joy....Everyone could see in the joy of Jesus's followers, that God is good news for the lost.[1]

The Beatitudes are tweets on how to be happy in every moment and season of life (see Luke 6:20–23, Matt 5:3–10). Jesus wants us all to flourish, to live in God's eternal love. He has come so that we "may have life, and have it abundantly" (John 10:10).

Did Jesus have fun? We know that when he was twelve years old, he joined the family caravan on a journey from Nazareth to Jerusalem to celebrate the Passover (see Luke 2:41–51). This was like a holiday because it was the celebration of a holy day. It involved traveling seventy miles over several days with cousins and kin in a

---

1. Pagola, *Jesus*, 284.

rambling extended family caravan, mostly on foot. Upon the completion of the Passover celebrations—which would have included worship, feasting, and shopping—this clan of grown-ups and children would have rambled back home.

Except that Jesus stayed behind. There must have been some fun and games going on with the young people, because it took Mary and Joseph three more days to find him. He was alone and homeless in the big city for four or five days. That sounds like quite an adventure.

After that episode, we only hear that the young Jesus grew in wisdom and stature, which implies he had an inquisitive mind and a growing body. We know that he learned to read and that he learned a trade, because he knew his Scriptures and he became a carpenter. At some stage, he left Nazareth and made a home for himself in Capernaum by the Sea of Galilee.

John the Baptist was Jesus's cousin and only a few months older than Jesus. He lived in wild places, making clothes out of camel hair, and living off locusts and wild honey. He challenged people to change their ways. He had a rock-star reputation. Not boring. At that time, Jesus would have been in his mid-twenties. Jesus went out into the wilderness for a time himself, ending up at the Jordan and seeking baptism from his cousin. This story is told in various ways in all four Gospels and suggests a consensus about Jesus as a young man: he was spirited, adventurous, and tested all the boundaries (cf. Matt 3–4; Mark 1; Luke 3—4; John 1).

So where did Jesus hang out? People may not have had the luxury of "hanging out" in those days, but Capernaum, thirty miles from Nazareth, was where Jesus made his home (see Mark 2:1; Matt 4:13; 13:54). Capernaum included Greek and Roman communities and would have been more cosmopolitan than Nazareth. Jesus probably spent time in the towns of Bethsaida and Magdala, which, like Capernaum, were also on the shores of the Sea of Galilee. These were, respectively, the hometowns of Simon Peter and Mary Magdalene. Simon Peter and his friends almost lived in their boats. A boat in those days would have been like a car today: it gave a young person a chance to spread their wings. The Sea of Galilee was their highway. Jesus gave his friends nicknames: Simon was "the Rock" and James and John were "the Sons of Thunder."

What was Jesus like? Jesus was an introvert who loved to go into the hills and into the wildernesses, the "thin places" where the barriers between the human and the divine are almost nonexistent. He found his Father in that solitude. But Jesus was also an extrovert, living in a cosmopolitan town, spending time with crowds and traveling in the company of a large group of disciples. He was charismatic and deeply compassionate. He was sharp-minded, constantly outwitting his critics. He was encouraging and forgiving. He would stop and chat with different women and men. He was committed to his calling. He was focused. He was brave and humble. He attracted crowds who flocked to hear him and to see what he would do next. Everybody wanted to be in the show.[2]

One crucial day, just after feeding the five thousand and walking on water, when he was teaching in Capernaum, Jesus challenged the crowd. He asked them if they were following him for the bread or for the Spirit of God. Were they there for the fun or for the kingdom of God? Sadly, as the gospel tells us, "Many of his disciples turned back and no longer went about with him" (John 6:66).

When Jesus entered Jerusalem on Palm Sunday at the very end of his public ministry, there was a large crowd shouting, singing, and celebrating him. Then the soldiers showed up and Jesus was taken into captivity. His closest companions abandoned him. He was crucified in a terrible death. But then, when the risen Lord came among them, they experienced unimaginable joy (Luke 24:41).

Not long ago, I was involved in the preparation of a diocesan pastoral plan that included consultation across the whole community. We visited three schools. In one of them we spent an hour with teenagers, trying to find out what they valued in the Church and what they wanted less and more of. They were pleasant enough, but not particularly engaged. We kept prodding them. Eventually one said, in a tentative tone of voice, "Do you really want to know what we think?" "Yes," we said, "that's what we came for." "Well," he said, "the music is terrible, the building is old and dusty, and the clothes they wear up there are frankly weird." It's an understatement to say that this young man found no joy in his local church.

Ask the young if they would prefer fun or joy or love. They would probably say they want it all. Jesus offers it all. It would help young people, then, if our churches looked less sourpuss, as Pope Francis famously put it,[3] and if they found our churches to be more welcoming and joyful. We may be the ones who make Jesus look boring.

---

2. See, e.g., Luke 5:1; 8:4, 42; 9:11; 11:29; 18:36; 14:25; 23:27; Mark 3:32; 5:24; 9:14; 10:1; Matt 4:24; 8:1, 18; 19:2; 20:29; 21:9.

3. Pope Francis, Apostolic Exhortation, *Evangelii Gaudium* [The Joy of the Gospel], §85.

4

DID JESUS HAVE A GIRLFRIEND?

"Of course, he did," said my learned friend Terry, almost dismissively, with a nod to Hebrews 4:15, "He was like us in all things but sin." Do we know? Or did he have a boyfriend? Did his heart throb? Some might think these are irreverent questions, but friendship and sexuality are part of our humanity and a constant preoccupation for young people. Dan Brown's *The Da Vinci Code* has also drawn attention to Jesus's relationship with Mary Magdalene and the possibility that they were lovers and had children. These are real questions for young people. Exploring them may help young people get to know Jesus better.

In the Gospels, Jesus talks about children playing a game in the marketplace where one group would sing a particular song and the other group had to act out the song (see Matt 11:16–17; Luke 7:32). He had probably played this game himself. And, from the story of Jesus getting lost on the caravan trip from Jerusalem to Nazareth, it seems that Jesus had a gaggle of relatives and friends when he was young. Perhaps he did have a girlfriend when he was young. We really do not know.

We know that Jesus cared for many women. Some of the women he healed were outcasts or neglected, yet Jesus noticed them and felt for them. There is the widow of Nain, the widow of Zarephath, the woman who touches the hem of his garment, the daughter of Jairus, the woman bent double, the woman caught in adultery, the Samaritan woman, the Syrophoenician woman, and the woman who was a public sinner. He brought a twelve-year-old girl back to life, saying "Little girl, get up," and he healed a crippled woman on the Sabbath, saying, "Woman, you are set free" (Mark 5:41–42; Luke 13:10–17). Jesus highlights both the plight and faith of women with stories about the unjust judge, the widow's mite, the lost coin, and the leaven in the bread.

The Gospels also tell us about the many women who followed Jesus.[1] This recognition of women might seem normal in our own time, albeit that patriarchy still exists

---

1. For more detail, see Pagola, "A Friend of Women," in *Jesus*, 207–30.

in many of our institutions. It is quite extraordinary, however, that so many women are noted and named in the stories about Jesus's ministry. These women not only listened to and ministered to him, but they were also numbered among his closest followers. They included Mary his mother, Mary the wife of Clopas (and the mother of James, Joses, and Judas), Mary Magdalene, Joanna the wife of Chuza, Susanna, Mary the mother of James and Salome, Martha and Mary of Bethany (the sisters of Lazarus), and the woman who washed the feet of Jesus with perfume. While there is some confusion about identities here—particularly of the woman who anointed Jesus's feet and the mother of James, Joses, and Judas—there can be no doubt that there was a group of women who were a constant element of his life.

Mary Magdalene, or Mary of Magdala, was one of two women, apart from his mother Mary, who were prominent in the life of Jesus. There is a third-century fragment that identifies Mary Magdalene as the companion of Jesus, but this is not a reliable source.[2] What we do know is that Mary Magdalene is mentioned twelve times in the Gospels—more than most of the apostles.[3] She is never mentioned as a prostitute or as anointing Jesus's feet with her hair. She was one among the group of women who supported Jesus and travelled with him to Jerusalem. She is named in all four Gospels as having been present at both the crucifixion and the resurrection. Given the proximity of Nazareth to Magdala, she may have known Jesus before he set out on his public ministry. Luke tells us, in passing, that seven demons had gone out of her. After Jesus's crucifixion, Mary Magdalene goes with other women to the tomb of Jesus to anoint his body. According to John, Mary is later alone outside the tomb weeping and seemingly bereft. Then, when she encounters the risen Jesus, he says to her, "Do not hold on to me," and sends her to tell his "brothers"—meaning the other disciples—the good news (John 20:17). In doing this, Mary Magdalene becomes the first person sent by Jesus to spread the good news of his resurrection. She becomes, in a sense, the first apostle. John's portrait of Mary indicates that she was very close to Jesus and that he bestowed on her a great honor.

Mary of Bethany was the second woman, apart from Mary his mother, who was close to Jesus. In the Gospel of Luke, we read of a woman called Martha, living in an unnamed village, who invites Jesus into her home, and how her sister, Mary, comes and sits at Jesus's feet—which may mean she sat as a student disciple rather than as

---

2. Fragments of the third-century "Gospel of Philip," produced by a fringe sect called Gnostics, report, "There were three who always walked with the Lord: Mary, his mother, and her sister, and Magdalene, the one who was called his companion," and that "Jesus kissed her."

3. Mary Magdalene is mentioned in Matt 27:56, 61; 28:1; Mark 15:40, 47; 16:1, 9; Luke 8:2; 24:10; John 19:25; 20:1, 18.

a lover—much to Martha's indignation. Yet Jesus commends Mary for choosing to be with him and admonishes poor Martha for worrying about the housework.

In the Gospel of John, we read a similar story about sisters called Mary and Martha, but this time we are told that they are sisters of Lazarus and that they are from Bethany. They have sent for Jesus because their brother is ill, but by the time Jesus arrives, poor Lazarus is dead. Martha scolds Jesus for taking so long to get there, but Mary falls at his feet weeping, which makes Jesus weep too. Then, in the following chapter we read the story of Jesus's second visit to the house of Lazarus, where Martha hosts a dinner to celebrate Lazarus's miraculous return to life. We are told that someone called Mary—presumably the sister of Martha and Lazarus—takes a pint of pure nard, pours it on Jesus's feet and wipes his feet with her hair, filling the house with the fragrance of the perfume. This intimate and uninhibited action shows that Mary of Bethany is deeply connected to Jesus. This is both an act of love and a preparation for Jesus's coming passion. Jesus does not push Mary of Bethany away, nor does he admonish her for the extravagance. He accepts her love and is moved by it. A similar event is described in Matthew and Mark, though with differences of detail. Their version concludes with Jesus saying, "wherever this good news is proclaimed in the whole world, what she has done will be told in remembrance of her" (Matt 26:13).[4] Jesus is thus portrayed as bestowing on Mary of Bethany another great honor. There is, here, an anticipation of the Last Supper and the washing of the feet, and Jesus's command to do these actions "in remembrance of me."

The Gospel stories always have a core of truth. Mary Magdalene and Mary of Bethany were not Jesus's lovers, nor were they married to him, but he receives their love and reciprocates it in an extraordinarily loving way: he immortalizes Mary of Magdala as a model apostle and Mary of Bethany as a model disciple. This love is both human and holy.

The Gospels also tell us that Jesus had special male friends, notably Simon Peter and an unnamed "beloved disciple" believed to be the youngest apostle, John. Simon Peter loved Jesus so much that he jumped into the sea to reach Jesus quickly. Jesus then asked Simon Peter three times if he loved him, to which he replied, "Lord, you know everything; you know that I love you" (John 21:7, 15–17). The "beloved disciple" is mentioned six times in the Gospel of John, though not in any of the other

---

4. See also John 12:1–2 and Mark 14:3–9. In Matthew and Mark, the woman is unnamed; the setting is in the house of Simon the Leper, but the location is still Bethany. There is a similar story of an unnamed prostitute who anoints Jesus's feet with her hair in the house of a Pharisee in Luke 7:36–50. Perhaps each of the Gospels is presenting the same basic story through its own lens.

Gospels. He was the one reclining next to Jesus at the Last Supper, the one who ran with Peter to the tomb after the crucifixion, and the one purported to be the author of the Gospel of John. In John's Gospel, only two people are mentioned as being both at the crucifixion and the resurrection. One is Mary Magdalene. The other is the "beloved disciple." Jesus's friendships were inclusive rather than exclusive.

We can conclude that Jesus was deeply loved by his friends—both women and men—and that Jesus felt the same love for them. While there are elements of romance and bromance in Jesus's closest friendships, the memory of the early Church is that Jesus gave himself completely to each and every person. If true love is self-giving, then infinite true love is infinitely self-giving. There is room for all, and no friendship that excluded others.

In John's Gospel, at the Last Supper, Jesus tells his disciples that they are his friends. The Greek word used for friends here, *philōn*, means more than just acquaintances. It means deep, lasting friends. Jesus says,

> No one has greater love than this, to lay down one's life for one's friends. You are my friends if you do what I command you....I have called you friends, because I have made known to you everything that I have heard from my Father. (John 15:13–15)

Finally, note that the Gospels are not biased against marriage. We know Peter was married because Jesus heals Peter's mother-in-law. There are many parables about brides and bridegrooms. When the disciples are accused of not fasting, Jesus compares himself to a bridegroom celebrating among his friends (see Matt 9:15; Mark 2:19; Luke 5:34). In the letters of St. Paul, as in the Book of Revelation, the Church is described as the Bride of Christ, such is his love for us (see Eph 5; 2 Cor 11; Rom 7; Rev 21). But there is nothing about Jesus being married.

So, from what we know, Jesus did not have a "girlfriend" in our contemporary sense of the word, but did his heart throb? Yes. His love was unbounded. In Catholic devotions, when we speak of the Sacred Heart of Jesus, we are speaking of Jesus's heart throb, his ecstatic love for each of us. Karl Rahner, one of the key theologians of the Second Vatican Council, describes the heart of Jesus as the heart of God in the world. So, if God is ecstatically in love with each of us, profoundly and uniquely, it follows that there are no limits or exclusions for Jesus's love for each of us. While in one sense there was no particular "special" love in Jesus's life, in another sense, we are all special loves in Jesus's life.

A PHILOSOPHICAL POSTSCRIPT ON FRIENDSHIP

The Greek philosopher Aristotle, who lived some three hundred years before Jesus, suggested that there are three types of friendship. First, there are what we might call practical friendships, where friends can be useful to each other and help each other, but where they are not usually seeking affection from each other. This often happens in the workplace. People get thrown together to collaborate. They become friends, but when they move jobs, they may lose touch with most of these workplace friends. These can be good friendships, but they are not deep. These are *accidental* friendships based on mutual *utility*.

Second, there are situations where we get thrown together and then develop friendships. This can happen to neighbors or at school, in a sporting team or in special interest groups like choirs. There can be a deeper bonding, here, but the relationships often come to an end when location or interests change. Sometimes these friendships turn into infatuations and then burn out, or they can become deeper friendships, with happy memories, but they may not last. These are *accidental* friendships based on mutual *pleasure*.

Finally, there are the friendships that last. These grow slowly, sometimes out of our accidental friendships. They endure over time, despite changes in life and work. They sometimes involve shared suffering, at other times shared joys. We open our hearts. These friendships have depth and intimacy. A true and lasting friend helps us to grow as a good person and gives us something of him or her and teaches us something about ourselves. They are not in the friendship for utility or pleasure. We learn how to be better persons from their enduring love and encouragement. These are *intentional* friendships based on *love*. This is the friendship that Jesus offers each of us, and the friendship that we find in the company of Jesus.

5

WAS JESUS TRULY HUMAN?

Yes, most certainly. Jesus was just like us: really, truly, fully human. He had to learn his way through life and when he was young, he asked lots of questions. He was not pretending to be human. Nor was he a hybrid—half human and half divine. Jesus was human just as much as we are human. He was one of us.

The story of Clark Kent/Superman provides a comparison. Superman is, according to the comic book, from the planet Krypton. His parents were Kryptonians. They looked human, but they had completely different powers. Although Superman identified with humanity and fell in love with a human, he was "not one of them," as his father, Jor-El, later told him. The point of Christian faith, however, is that Jesus *is one of us*, fully human.

What does *human* mean? And how can we be so sure?

The word *human* has two meanings. First, *human* has a scientific meaning. A human being, distinct from other animals, belongs to the genus "homo" and the species "sapiens." While human biology is not greatly different from that of other mammals, and while human beings are diverse in external appearance, they are all equally distinguished in their advanced capacity for speech, imagination, creativity, and thought. Human beings are born from a mix of male and female human chromosomes. This is what a human being is as a scientific specimen, as an "object."

Second, and equally relevant, the word *human* has an existential meaning. A human being is a person, someone alive in a particular time and place, someone who loves and hopes, who has a sense of right and wrong, who is vulnerable and mortal, who experiences themself as both body and spirit, and who finds belonging in relationships and communities. A human being is more than a scientific specimen. Existentially, a human being is a person or "subject."

The Gospels point to Jesus being human, both biologically and existentially. We are told that Jesus is born of a woman. He grew as a child normally grows—he lived at home, he had kin and, on one occasion, he seemed to have run away from his parents. He probably made some innocent mistakes. As an adult, he grew in wisdom and knowledge, he learned carpentry, he knew the Scriptures, he prayed, he sought out his place in life, he left home, he cared, he dreamed, he created elegant stories, he connected people together, he taught, healed, and worked wonders. He hoped and wept, he felt hungry and thirsty, he liked company and solitude, he suffered pain, he felt betrayed, and he felt abandoned. He got thirsty, he bled, and he died. He is identified in the Scriptures as being human. For example:

> "Jesus increased in wisdom and in years, and in divine and human favor" (Luke 2:52).

> "Is not this the carpenter, the son of Mary and brother of James and Joses and Judas and Simon, and are not his sisters here with us?" (Mark 6:3).

> "Jesus, tired out by his journey, was sitting by the well" (John 4:6).

> "Jesus began to weep" (John 11:35).

> "There is...one mediator between God and humankind, Christ Jesus, himself human" (1 Tim 2:5).

What complicates the question about Jesus being human, however, is that there are several passages in the New Testament that unambiguously declare that Jesus's birth was not the result of a normal human conception, and that Jesus is also the Son of God. For example:

> "In the beginning was the Word, and the Word was with God, and the Word was God....And the Word became flesh and lived among us, and we have seen his glory, the glory as of a father's only son, full of grace and truth" (John 1:1, 14).

> "Now the birth of Jesus the Messiah took place in this way. When his mother Mary had been engaged to Joseph, but before they lived together, she was found to be with child from the Holy Spirit" (Matt 1:18).

> "But when the fullness of time had come, God sent his Son, born of a woman" (Gal 4:4).

While these passages suggest something exceptional about Jesus, note that these texts equally insist on his humanity. They declare that Jesus was born of a woman, becoming flesh among us. The Nicene Creed thus declares that Jesus was both true God from true God and made a human being. The original Greek word in the Creed—*enanthropaisanta*—has *anthropos*, or "human," at its heart, just as the Latin translation has *homo factus est*, or "was made a human being." The current official Catholic English translation of the Greek and Latin is, unfortunately, "and was made man." A more helpful and theologically accurate translation would be: "and was made human."

Existentially, Jesus is described in the Gospels as a human person formed in relationships with other human persons. As one writer observes, "Always he is in society, in company, loved, helped. Living in a society of living people, from which he does not emerge as a solitary man. Sharing needs and desires with mortals."[1]

Young people should be satisfied that Jesus really existed, and that Jesus was fully human. Some will ask, however, questions like "How could Mary be a virgin?" and "Was Jesus really God?" and "If Jesus was really God, how could he be really human too?" Read on!

---

1. Luce Irigaray, "The Crucified One," in her *Marine Lover of Friedrich Nietzsche* (New York: Columbia University Press, 1991), 182.

6

HOW COULD MARY BE A VIRGIN?

How could Mary be the mother of Jesus and still be a virgin? Young people are at a stage of life where they are learning about, and interested in, sexuality. This can be a confusing time.

Mary, the mother of Jesus, asks the same question herself. When God sends a message to her—an angel rather than a tweet—saying that she would have a son who would be the Messiah, she protests, "How can this be, since I am a virgin?" (Luke 1:34). She is described in the Greek text of the Gospel as *parthenon*, which means young woman, or a young woman of marriageable age, or a young woman who has never had sex. Perhaps "maiden" is a better translation than "virgin," though the meanings are interchangeable.[1] She may even have been a teenager herself.

Only two of the Gospels—Matthew and Luke—tell us about Jesus's conception and birth. While they differ in several respects, they clearly agree that Mary was a virgin, betrothed to Joseph, and who, before they were married and had been together, became pregnant (cf. Matt 1:18, Luke 1:26–27). When Mary is described in the Gospels as a virgin, however, the term has more than biological significance. Mary's virginity should be seen as a fundamental element of her extraordinary humanity, given her unconditional openness to God. The human heart seeks infinite love, and to be fully human and to be fully alive is to be at one with God. Even though she questions the angel and is no meek, passive person, when the angel responds to Mary's question by saying that nothing is impossible for God, she replies, "Here am I, the servant of the Lord; let it be with me according to your word" (Luke 1:38). Mary is a young woman of intelligent faith who completely trusts an infinite God.

Mary's trust in God never changed. She was with Jesus through his ministry and at his crucifixion. In the Gospels, she is referred to as "Mary, the mother of Jesus" or

---

1. The words *parthenon* and *parthenou*, both used by Luke, relate to the Greek word for "virgin." Matthew quotes Isaiah—"the virgin shall conceive and bear a son"—using the Greek word *parthenos* as a translation of the Hebrew *almah* used by Isaiah, which means "young woman."

"Mary, his mother" or the like. After Jesus's death and resurrection, at the start of the Acts of the Apostles, we find Mary at the heart of the community, as if mother of the early Church.

Mary's titles have evolved as the Church has grown. From the end of the second century, Mary was celebrated as Mother of God and Virgin Mother. Later, from the fifth century on, we find Mary described as Ever Virgin. St. Augustine, for example, wrote that Mary "remained a virgin in conceiving her Son, a virgin in giving birth to him, a virgin in carrying him, a virgin in nursing him at her breast, always a virgin."[2] These titles are worthy titles. Crucially, they are also theological in that they are not so much *about Mary* as *about Jesus*. They affirm that Jesus was both entirely human and uniquely divine.

Some theologians suggest that "Ever Virgin" is primarily a title that reflects the identity of a person rather than a biological fact. For example, at a more trivial level, the boxer Muhammad Ali has the title "the greatest." This reflects his identity. He remained the greatest long after he lost his final fight. Scientifically, he is an ex-boxer. Existentially, his identity transcends space and time. So also, it is argued, Mary's titles forever reflect her momentous openness to God.

Others argue that the Church's celebration of Mary as Ever Virgin not only seems a rejection of human sexuality but also puts Mary on a lofty pedestal out of reach of ordinary humans. The Gospels paint a different picture. She rejoices in becoming a mother, she celebrates her cousin's pregnancy, she is perhaps a refugee in Egypt, perhaps homeless for a time in Bethlehem, she may have become frustrated with some of her son's activities, she makes sure a wedding feast at Cana is a spectacular success by getting Jesus to do something about the supply of wine, and she watches her son die a horrible death. No pedestals here. The Second Vatican Council (1962–65) thus issued a caution about how we celebrate Mary:

> This most Holy Synod...exhorts theologians and preachers of the divine word to abstain zealously both from all gross exaggerations as well as from petty narrow-mindedness in considering the singular dignity of the Mother of God.[3]

In summary, "What the Catholic faith believes about Mary is based on what it believes about Christ."[4] In other words, Mary is important because Jesus is important. We

---

2. St. Augustine, Sermon 186. See *Catechism of the Catholic Church*, §§508–11.

3. This quotation is from "The Blessed Virgin Mary, Mother of God in the Mystery of Christ and the Church," chap. 8 in *Lumen Gentium: Dogmatic Constitution on the Church*, §§66–67.

4. *Catechism*, §487.

venerate Mary because, from among us all, she is both the one most open to God and the one closest to Jesus.

Is it too much to believe that Jesus's birth was extraordinary? If we can believe something extraordinary happened in the resurrection of Jesus, we can also believe something extraordinary happened in the birth of Jesus. Extraordinary events demand extraordinary descriptions. Furthermore, we can anticipate that something extraordinary will happen in us if, like Mary, we open ourselves to God's love. We will find Jesus alive among us, just as Jesus became alive in Mary. It is because of her extraordinary trust in God and her motherhood of Jesus that Mary should be famed and celebrated. If we are to find humanity in Jesus, we must also maintain the humanity in Mary.

A SCIENTIFIC POSTSCRIPT ON VIRGIN BIRTH

Some young people may have difficulty accepting the Gospel testimony that Mary was a virgin when Jesus was conceived, not only because it seems a rejection of sexuality but also because scientifically it seems impossible. While the Gospel accounts should be seen as products of the experience of the early Church, rather than judged on contemporary science, questions about scientific impossibility must be considered. In other words, while our beliefs might transcend science, they must be tested against science. For example, Church authorities have slowly come to accept that contemporary accounts of creation are scientifically true and yet also complement, rather than conflict with, theological accounts of creation.

Regarding the doctrine of the perpetual virginity of Mary, it might be argued that it is scientifically possible for a woman to become pregnant and to bear a child without losing her biological virginity. This could be achieved through artificial insemination and caesarean delivery. Of course, I am not suggesting this happened in Mary's case. My point is to reflect on what "scientifically impossible" can mean. It is unwise to settle theological questions with scientific arguments. Biological concerns miss the theological points that the birth of Jesus is a gift of God and that Mary's virginity is her complete openness to God.

There is, however, some other scientific research that might be noted here. It is scientifically possible for a woman to become pregnant without any external fertilization. This is because the male Y chromosome is derived from the female X chromosome and is one of the fastest evolving parts of the human genome. Thus, in many species, including sharks and chickens, female eggs have produced offspring without any male participation. While this so-called parthenogenesis (or virgin birth) often results in birth abnormalities and is unknown for mammals in the wild, there are reported instances of scientifically induced parthenogenesis in rabbits, mice, and monkeys and, more recently, human embryos. On this evidence, it is scientifically possible that something extraordinary happened in Mary's pregnancy, namely an extraordinary step in the evolution of the X chromosome. Once again, though, we should focus on the theological point: the extraordinary thing that happened in Mary's pregnancy was that God came among us.

7

DID JESUS HAVE BROTHERS AND SISTERS?

The young person asking this question may be a careful reader of the Scriptures or may have noted, in 2002, that archaeologists had discovered a two-thousand-year-old ossuary—a limestone box of bones—with the Aramaic inscription, "James, son of Joseph, Brother of Jesus."[1] More likely, though, the person was influenced by the spate of blogs on the bloodlines of Jesus prompted by Dan Brown's novel *The Da Vinci Code.* Brown had included speculation about Jesus having brothers and sisters in the early drafts of his novel, but he later removed them from the final drafts because the evidence was so light.[2]

This question could also be about how to relate to Jesus, because adolescents often relate more to their peers and sisters and brothers than they do to their mothers and fathers, or because some children have no brothers or sisters yet want to have a sibling to whom they can feel close. If so, this is also an existential question about the sort of person Jesus was when he was growing up.

Finally, this could be a challenging question because Christian denominations hold varying beliefs about whether Jesus had sisters or brothers or not. Young people might be confused about what to believe. Catholics and Orthodox Christians believe that Mary was ever a virgin, and that Mary had no other children. Some Protestants believe that, after Jesus was born, and as the Bible seems to suggest, Mary and Joseph had children together, and that these are brothers and sisters of Jesus.

So, did Jesus have brothers and sisters? The Gospels seem to suggest that he did. For example, when Jesus returns to his hometown of Nazareth, the people know him and ask among themselves, "Is not this the carpenter, the son of Mary and brother

---

1. While the ossuary itself seems authentic, the inscription is considered a forgery.
2. See Dan Brown's own vlog from 2019, https://www.facebook.com/DanBrown/videos/472052080013230.

of James and Joses and Judas and Simon, and are not his sisters here with us?" (Mark 6:3).[3] We also read about the brothers of the Lord in several other verses of the New Testament (see Luke 8:19; John 2:12; 7:5; Gal 1:19; Acts 1:14). And why would Jesus be called Mary's firstborn son (Luke 2:7) if she only had one child? Some scholars see this as further evidence that Jesus was a thoroughly normal human being with brothers and sisters.

Other scholars are more cautious. This is because the Gospel stories would have started out in Hebrew and Aramaic, and because these languages make no simple distinctions between brother/sister/cousin/kin/friend. The word *brother* could be used more loosely in Hebrew, as it often is among friends and gangs today. It is possible that the original Aramaic meanings were lost in translation to the written Greek. On top of this, both Matthew and Mark tell us that Mary the mother of Jesus had a sister (or cousin) called Mary of Clopas (see John 19:25), who had sons called James and Joses (see Matt 27:56, Mark 15:40). These are the same names given to Jesus's "brothers" noted in Mark 6:3 above, so it is more than likely that James and Joses were Jesus's cousins and not his brothers. Finally, if Mary did have other sons, why does the passage of Mark about Jesus's brothers say that Jesus is *the* son of Mary" rather than "*a* son of Mary"?

Some traditions explain the Gospel texts about Jesus's brothers and sisters by suggesting that these were children of Mary's husband, Joseph, from an earlier marriage. The Orthodox and Catholic churches, however, have long taught that Mary remained Ever Virgin and that Jesus was her only child. Reformers like Martin Luther and John Wesley agreed, and Lutheran and Anglican churches have held the same view.

We can say that Jesus's family history was as wonderful and complicated as any other human family. We can be confident that Jesus grew up with family and kin and a gaggle of friends about him. We know this because he got lost with his kinfolk (*syngenes*, meaning "blood relatives") on his trip to Jerusalem when he was twelve years old.

Finally, there is a remarkable event reported in three of the Gospels when Jesus's mother and family appear to become concerned about his behavior. It's as though Jesus has gone too far, and they are worried about him. The story goes like this:

---

3. This story is repeated in Matt 13:55. The Greek word *adelphoi* used in the Gospels could be translated as "brothers and sisters" or just as "brothers," given that sometimes the word *adelphai*, meaning "sisters," is explicitly used, e.g., in the quote from Mark 6:3.

Then his [Jesus's] mother and his brothers came; and standing outside, they sent to him and called him. A crowd was sitting around him; and they said to him, "Your mother and your brothers and sisters are outside, asking for you." And he replied, "Who are my mother and my brothers?" And looking at those who sat around him, he said, "Here are my mother and my brothers! Whoever does the will of God is my brother and sister and mother." (Mark 3:31–35)[4]

In this sense, Jesus truly did claim many sisters and brothers, and Jesus invites us now, today, to be his sister or brother too, and to walk with him on his way. With Jesus, we are equally children of a loving God. We are all sisters and brothers of Jesus.

---

4. See also Matt 12:46 and Luke 8:19. John tells a story about Jesus visiting Capernaum with his mother and brothers (John 2:12).

8

DID JESUS REALLY WALK ON WATER?

Did Neil Armstrong really walk on the moon? Skeptics claim that it was fake and that all the footage was shot in a studio by Stanley Kubrick. There is enough context and enough evidence, however, to convince most people that Armstrong really did walk on the moon. Did Jesus really walk on water? If he did, Jesus certainly is someone very special. We need to consider the context and the evidence. A careful investigation will help us understand the Gospel stories. Their focus is not so much on Jesus's miracles as on how special Jesus is.

Technically, Jesus did not walk on water. According to the Greek text of this story in all three Gospels, Jesus walked not on the water but "on the sea" (*epi tên thalassan*), meaning the Sea of Galilee. Furthermore, it is Peter who is described as trying to walk "on the water" (*epi ta hydata*) when he steps out of the boat to go to Jesus before he loses faith and sinks (see Matt 14:25–29; Mark 6:48–49; John 6:19). The same two Greek words are used in all three Gospels. Is a point being made? Perhaps walking on the sea is different from walking on water.

If you have ever experienced being out at sea in a small boat, especially when it is dark and waves are breaking over the boat, when the wind is driving spray into your eyes like needles, and you can see nothing but chaos, then you will understand this Gospel story. It is about being helpless in the face of violent forces. It is about the fear of death. It is about being abandoned by God. A good way to begin answering this question in a class could be to ask if any of the young people have been out in a small boat on a stormy sea and what it felt like, or to ask students to imagine what it might feel like.

It happened to me once. I had joined what was meant to be a pleasant afternoon of sailing with two companions in a small open boat. We set out from Cohasset Cove, south of Boston, and sailed into the North Atlantic Ocean. Unexpectedly, a cold storm rushed toward us from the eastern horizon. We were perhaps a mile from the coast, maybe less. The sky turned a violent dark charcoal color. The wind started screaming through the rigging. The rain was piercing through us. The yacht was leaning almost sideways, with water washing at its sides. It was like a scene out of Moby Dick. Our skipper, David, however, seemed unafraid. It helped that he had once been an international yachtsman. "We can't head back into the harbor," he said, "because we can only sail sideways to the wind, but these squalls usually disappear as quickly as they come." For half an hour or so, filled with terror, we surfed our way up and down the coast. The third member of our party came from central India and had never been out on the ocean before. He sat calmly in the middle of the boat, a smile upon his face. Eventually, the wind eased, the sun came out, and we tacked our way back into Cohasset.

There was yet a twist to the tale. The wind dropped completely. The tide turned and a strong current rushed down the channel and out to sea again. Where we were, on the edge of the channel, the water was not too deep. I was just tall enough to jump out, get my feet on the sandbank, and pull the boat to safety. I walked *in* the water. Later, in the retelling of our adventures, the man from India joked about me walking *under* the water.

There are many sailing stories like this; people are at the mercy of the elements, they fear they may drown, and they survive. Details may get exaggerated, but the core of each story remains the same. Often the storm gets bigger over time and the waves get higher with each telling. The stories about Jesus walking on the sea are similar because there are several variations. We need to read them all to get the meaning of the miracle.

Initially, we find almost the same story in three of the Gospels (cf. Matt 14:22–33; Mark 6:45–52; John 6:15–21). Immediately after the feeding of the five thousand, Jesus sends the crowd home, for it is getting late. He then goes into the hills to be by himself for a while. The disciples set out in a boat to cross the lake. Late into the night a strong wind is blowing against them and waves break into their boat.

They are rowing and getting nowhere, but they are experienced sailors. Though they are being buffeted by the wind, there is no mention in any of these three stories of the disciples becoming anxious *because of the storm*. It is only when they see what seems like a ghost—a spectre that just might be Jesus walking toward them—that they get scared. They had no torches, and it was a stormy night. What could they have seen? The same Greek word meaning "frightened" or "terrified" is used in all three Gospels. This vision, who might be Jesus, then says, "It is I; do not be afraid."

The same Greek words are used in all three Gospels. Given these consistencies, it seems reasonable to suggest that we have the core of an actual event. Something happened that night to produce a story that the disciples, many of them being fishermen and sailors, would tell repeatedly.

There are, however, significant differences of detail in each Gospel. Mark says the boat was "out on the sea" and that Jesus, from the hills, could see them struggling against the wind. Then the disciples see Jesus in the storm and, though at first it looked like he was going to pass them by, Jesus gets into the boat with them, and the wind then ceases. Matthew's version is quite different. He says the boat was "far from land," but he may have been embellishing the story, because he alone adds the story about Peter trying to walk on water toward Jesus. John says they had rowed about three or four miles and that immediately after they saw Jesus—who does not get into the boat—they "reached the land toward which they were going."

To explain this variation, the stories must be set in a wider context. Earlier in three Gospels there are somewhat similar stories of a journey at sea and a violent storm (cf. Matt 8:23–27; Mark 4:35–41; Luke 8:22–25). In these stories, when the disciples set off for the other side of the lake, Jesus is already in the boat and sound asleep. When the storm arises, the disciples are terrified not because they see Jesus like a ghost walking on the sea, but because they are in fear of perishing. In these stories, Jesus *tells the water to be calm*, whereas in the later stories he *tells the disciples not to be afraid*.

The two sets of stories are like two acts of a long play. They slowly reveal who Jesus is. The first act—the first set of stories—occurs very early in Jesus's ministry. He calms the storm and the disciples wonder what kind of man this can be, because even the wind and the sea obey him. They possibly remembered that the Creator God is the one who "made the storm be still, and the waves of the sea were hushed" (Ps 107[106]:29). In the second act, when Jesus walks on the sea later in his ministry, there are different endings. Matthew, typically, has Peter saying, "Truly you are the Son of God," while Mark and John add no immediate comment, except that the disciples were "utterly astounded." It seems that Jesus is now challenging his disciples: the full truth of Jesus's extraordinary identity is emerging. Things are about to get serious. Jesus may save their lives, but he is soon to give his own life.

And then there is a third act, another story about Jesus and boats and disciples that is also relevant here. According to John, after Jesus's crucifixion, at a time when the disciples felt despondent and at a loss, they returned to the Sea of Galilee for a spot of fishing, as men still do. They were out all night but caught nothing, as still happens today. Then, early in the morning, they see a stranger on the shore. He tells them to cast their nets one more time. They catch a huge haul of fish. John continues,

> That disciple whom Jesus loved said to Peter, "It is the Lord!" When Simon Peter heard that it was the Lord, he put on some clothes, for he was naked, and jumped into the sea. But the other disciples came in the boat, dragging the net full of fish, for they were not far from the land, only about a hundred yards off. (John 21:7–8)

In other words, from about a hundred yards offshore, Peter was able to jump into the water and wade toward Jesus. He walked in the water. John later notes that none of the disciples dared ask Jesus, "Who are you?" They know now, once and for all, this is the risen Lord coming to be with them and to share his love with them in the breakfast he has prepared.

In the context of the Gospels, then, the stories of Jesus walking on the sea involve three acts. We have boats, nighttime, fear, confusion, disappointment, Jesus being hard to recognize, people on the water, and people in the water. In the meantime, the fearful disciples are transformed from wondering who this man is (act 1), to being utterly astounded and saying nothing (act 2), to knowing Jesus as the risen Lord (act 3). There is an abiding message here. The early Church believed, as Christians continue to believe today, that Jesus will be watching us, walking with us, even quietly sailing through the storm with us. He is extraordinary. He is the Messiah.

Very good, but did Jesus really walk on the sea? In the dark of night, with water spraying in their eyes, this is what the disciples saw and believed. That is what the Gospel testifies. We also know that waves become most dangerous when the sea becomes shallow, and that the Sea of Galilee is shallow in many parts, shallow enough to wade a hundred yards to shore. The boat may have been in great danger and yet, at the same time, close enough to the shore for Jesus to wade out on the sea and help bring the exhausted rowers to safety. Or perhaps Jesus really did walk on the water. What is certain is that the disciples were out on the lake, the situation was precarious, and Jesus was keeping an eye on them and came to be with them.

None of this is meant to imply that the miracle of walking on the sea didn't really happen. In one way or another, Jesus was seen to walk on the sea. But the real question coming to the minds of the disciples at this stage of Jesus's ministry is about something far more dramatic. Could Jesus really be the Messiah?

I have often heard parents say that they would walk over hot coals for their children. I have seen a father dive into raging surf to save a struggling daughter. In my darkest times, I find the risen Jesus very close. He appears from nowhere because he is always present. He can walk on water for me. That is the miracle of his love.

9

DID JESUS WORK ALL THOSE OTHER MIRACLES?

It is grand to have all these questions, but did Jesus really feed thousands of people with a few loaves and fishes? Did he make the blind see, help the lame walk, heal lepers, bring back people from the dead? Did Jesus actually work all these miracles? By definition, aren't miracles scientifically impossible? Or was Jesus a great magician? Or a con artist? Or are these stories made up?

One question at a time, please. First, the easy ones: no, Jesus was neither a magician nor a con artist. We know this because he refused to produce signs from heaven for those who asked for them (see Matt 12:38–39; Luke 11:29–30), and he never worked miracles to make life easier for himself. He was not about showing off or self-aggrandizement. He asked people not to talk about his healings, and he tried to escape the adulation of the crowds. He challenged people to see beyond the miracles and acknowledge the coming of the kingdom of God among them.

Second, regarding the hard ones, did Jesus really work all those other miracles? The Gospels explicitly refer to Jesus's reputation as a miracle worker (see Matt 21:21; Mark 6:5, 56; 9:39; Luke 23:8; John 4:54; 12:18). So, as far as the people were concerned, Jesus really did do all those miracles. They were signs of God's blessing. They fulfilled the prophecy about the Christ, God's anointed one: the lame will walk; the blind will see; and captives will be set free.

The knowledge-hungry student will most likely interrupt at this stage. "But did Jesus *really* do miracles? Did they *actually* happen?" Press the pause button and explain what *miracle* means in the Gospels. We use the word today to talk about unexpected cures or against-the-odds sporting moments. Today *miracle* means a highly improbable or impossible happening where modern science is often the judge. Winning the lottery is not really a miracle, though it might feel like one. Recovering from cancer may or may not be a miracle. The birth of a baby seems miraculous, day after day, but from a scientific perspective it is simply nature at work. The word *miracle* suggests wonder. In Christianity, a miracle is a highly improbable or impossible happening that involves and reveals the love and power of God.

So, we can say that many of Jesus's miracles entailed the highly improbable, but not the scientifically or medically impossible. Consider, for example, all his healing miracles. Nearly one fifth of the Gospels is about Jesus healing people: lepers; demoniacs (mentally ill people); deaf, blind, and lame people; a paralyzed servant; a mother-in-law with a fever; a man with a withered hand; the dead son of a widow; a dying daughter; a hemorrhaging woman; epileptics; a man with dropsy (edema); a cut ear; an infirmity (rheumatoid arthritis?); and so on. There are also reports of several mass healings where people waited for days to be touched by Jesus. He was quite a clinician, but it was all in a day's work, as Matthew writes:

> Jesus went throughout Galilee, teaching in their synagogues and proclaiming the good news of the kingdom and curing every disease and every sickness among the people. So his fame spread throughout all Syria, and they brought to him all the sick, those who were afflicted with various diseases, and pains, demoniacs, epileptics, and paralytics, and he cured them. (Matt 4:23–24)

Most of these healings are possible today, whether through Western medicine, alternative healing, or even faith healing. There is no reason to dismiss these Gospel stories as fabrications. Jesus made these things happen. The consistent testimony of the time was, as the historian Josephus put it, that Jesus was "a doer of wonderful works."[1] These healing stories are possible, if improbable, so why not believe that Jesus really did them? Perhaps he did not work all these miracles in the precise details that are reported, but I believe he really did work miracles, and that is the core truth of the Gospel stories.[2]

But what about the scientifically impossible miracles? Surely, it is scientifically impossible to walk on water, or to turn water into wine, or to raise the dead back to life. Could these stories be exaggerations or retrospective constructions? Perhaps Jesus seemed like he was walking on the sea. Perhaps he knew his friends were good drinkers and had secretly arranged for some extra wine. Perhaps the people Jesus

---

1. See Pagola, *Jesus*, 474.
2. For more on how to read the Gospel stories, see chaps. 19—20 in part 2.

raised back to life just needed some resuscitation. Perhaps the task of telling salvation history justifies some stretching of historical facts.

Take care. To follow this path of perhaps after perhaps is to risk falling into three traps. First, it falls into the trap of having a naïve view of science as possessing absolute truth, because science can never give absolute certainty about what is possible in the material world. Even contemporary physics subverts our commonsense views of the laws of motion and the reality of space and time. Second, rejecting Jesus's miracles falls into the trap of reducing our world to a limited, disenchanted, material reality, where only material objects count, where everything can be explained, and where there is no room for the extraordinary, transcendent, or enchanted. Love and art, however, tell us there is more to strive for and challenge us to open our horizons. Third, "perhaps after perhaps" falls into the trap of making humans the arbiters of what is possible and what is real. Surely, it is reasonable to allow nature, and especially a loving creator of nature, to be the arbiter of what is possible.

I am not arguing here against science. Nor am I arguing for what is called an "interventionist God," which implies that God lives somewhere outside our universe and occasionally and capriciously jumps in and changes the course of nature. Rather, I am inviting you to imagine what it might be like to live in a world where there is both human freedom and the loving presence of God. The idea of a miracle, in the religious sense, entails both divine respect for the autonomy of nature and divine concern for creation coming to the fullness of life.[3]

My view is that the birth of Jesus, seen as the incarnation of the Divine, is a uniquely unprecedented event in nature. It is, if you like, a major step in evolution. It can entail unprecedented things. My response to the difficult question about miracles is this: Yes, something did happen, and the miracles are not just exaggerations, strokes of luck, or extraordinary coincidences. The miracles are mighty works and wonders and signs, and they attest that Jesus is the promised Messiah. There is plenty of evidence, and there is a context. Can you believe that? I do.

A SCIENTIFIC POSTSCRIPT ON MIRACLES

If a miracle entails a scientifically impossible event, does this mean God breaks the laws of nature? The answer is no for three reasons. First, as noted above, the

---

3. For questions about God's relationship to nature and why God allows good people to suffer, see the first book in this series: John Honner, *Does God Like Being God? And Other Tricky Questions about God* (Mahwah, NJ: Paulist Press, 2019).

laws of nature as formulated by science are never absolute and, indeed, are often evolving. For example, Newton's Laws of Motion have proved to be inadequate—and sometimes wrong at the atomic level—and have been replaced by Einstein's theory of relativity. Second, the order of nature is created by God, rather than the other way around and so, third, everything that happens in nature is a manifestation or epiphany of God. In other words, when a miracle happens, our narrow view of nature is challenged. God is not intervening in a fixed order so much as revealing a more profound order. This is how science progresses.

Paul Dirac, one of the great physicists of the twentieth century, regarded a beautiful theory as more important than an experimental result. He declared, "It is more important to have beauty in one's equations than to have them fit experiment."[4] John Polkinghorne, a Cambridge professor of physics, goes further:

> Science cannot exclude the possibility that, on particular occasions, God does particular unprecedented things. After all, God is the ordainer of the laws of nature, not someone who is subjected to them. However, precisely because they are *divine* laws, simply to overturn them would be for God to act against God, which is absurd. The theological question is, does it make sense to suppose that God has acted in a new way?...God can't be capricious, but must be utterly consistent. However, consistency is not the same as dreary uniformity. In unprecedented circumstances, God can do unexpected things. Yet there will always have to be a deep underlying consistency which makes it intelligible....The search for this consistency is the *theological* challenge of miracle.[5]

In faith, this "underlying consistency" is God's enduring and unconditional love.

---

4. Paul Dirac, "The Evolution of the Physicist's Picture of Nature," *Scientific American* 208, no. 5 (1963).
5. John Polkinghorne, *Quarks, Chaos and Christianity* (New York: Crossroad, 1994, 2005), 100.

10

WAS JESUS A COWBOY? A REBEL? A PRIEST? A PROPHET?

José Pagola says that "Jesus is the best that humanity has ever produced. He is the most admirable power of light and hope available to us as human being....It also hurts to hear him described in routine, worn-out language."[1] Young people can help us refresh our language about Jesus and perhaps help us be more precise.

This first question, "Was Jesus a cowboy?" arose on a train trip across the United States of America. We were chugging eastward on the California Zephyr, perhaps in Nevada. There on our right was a small, weathered shed with a faded sign above the door, "The Cowboy Church." It was humble. Beautiful. I later discovered that there are cowboy churches scattered across America, even in Australia. They refer more to a style of worship than to a theology of Jesus.

There are a few songs celebrating Jesus being a cowboy, and there is a wry humor in identifying Jesus as a cowboy. While the Gospels indicate that Jesus was a good shepherd who cared for his sheep, the cowboys point out that Jesus was born in a cow manger whereas the sheep were out in the hills. And Jesus drifted from town to town, just like a cowboy. And on Palm Sunday he rode bareback on an unbroken colt, just like a cowboy. He must have been a cowboy. I think that Jesus loves that cowboy church because of its simplicity and honesty, but Jesus wasn't a cowboy! Jesus is much more than a cowboy, but perhaps there is some cowboy in Jesus.

There are songs about Jesus being a Capricorn, a Democrat, and a Terrorist, but he is more than any of these. There are many other claims for Jesus. These all run the risk of making him in our own image. That makes us feel good about ourselves because—surprise, surprise—we can be happy that we are just like this Jesus we have imagined for ourselves, and he is just like us. The stories of the saints, however, tell

---

1. Pagola, *Jesus*, 15.

us that we will find more about Jesus when we step out of our own world and into a completely different world, God's world. We find Jesus's features in the face of our neighbor, especially in the face of the poor, sick, and outcast.

Christians believe that Jesus is alive now, and *who Jesus is now* is the same person as *who Jesus was then*. So, what was Jesus like *then*? According to the Gospels, as well as being a traveling teacher and healer, Jesus was an inspiring leader and a liberator. The Spirit of God was on him and in him. He seemed to belong more among the prophets than the priests. The Gospel of Luke, drawing on the prophet Isaiah, has Jesus beginning his ministry in these terms:

> The Spirit of the Lord is upon me,
> because he has anointed me
> to bring good news to the poor.
> He has sent me to proclaim release to the captives
> and recovery of sight to the blind,
> to let the oppressed go free,
> to proclaim the year of the Lord's favor. (Luke 4:18–19)

The first lines describe Jesus as a preacher, teacher, healer, and liberator, and especially as the anointed one of God. This is who Jesus was and is. The last line of the passage is particularly important because it locates Jesus at a point where God's eternity and love become explicitly manifest in every moment of human time.

Jesus was certainly in the prophetic tradition. A prophet is not simply someone who tells the future, but rather an inspiring visionary, open to the Spirit of God, who hopes in God and speaks for God, who scarifies the hypocritical and the hard-hearted. A prophet is driven by God's Spirit. In this sense, Jesus is the ultimate prophet, conceived by the Spirit, driven by the Spirit. In biblical terms, Jesus is best described as the anointed one of God—the Messiah or the Christ—the one full of God's Spirit. He was an extraordinary prophet.

Three of the Gospels record an instructive scene where Jesus's emerging identity is recognized as being more than a prophet. The Gospel of Mark, for example, states,

> Jesus went on with his disciples to the villages of Caesarea Philippi; and on the way he asked his disciples, "Who do people say that I am?" And they answered him, "John the Baptist; and others, Elijah; and still others, one

of the prophets." He asked them, "But who do you say that I am?" Peter answered him, "You are the Messiah." (Mark 8:27–29)[2]

While Jesus is in the line of the prophets, then, he is much more than a prophet: he is the Christ.

Was Jesus a rebel? By all accounts Jesus challenged authorities and set people free. He invited people to come into the kingdom of God. *Kingdom* is an old-fashioned and gendered word, and today many prefer to speak of the "reign" of God. Perhaps we could also translate the *kingdom of God* as "the regime of God." This would mean that Jesus was about "regime change." And regime change is the core business of rebels.

Jesus certainly broke through barriers. He said he had come to cast fire upon the earth (see Luke 12:49). He was a public figure of great concern to the Jewish and Roman authorities. He could be combative and dangerous,[3] and was seen as a threat to civil and religious authorities. His actions certainly led to his arrest, imprisonment, and crucifixion. But if he was something of a rebel, he was neither a political activist nor a militant terrorist. He was countercultural in ways that were both radical and conservative. He had not come to abolish the law or the prophets, but to fulfill them (see Matt 5:17).

The Church teaches that Jesus the Christ has a threefold identity as priest, prophet, and king. This is partly because, in the biblical stories, the great priests, prophets, and kings were all anointed by God, and so the one most fully anointed, the Christ, must in some respects also be priest, prophet, and king. The Gospels, however, barely use these titles. Jesus is never explicitly identified as a priest, and the Gospels declare Jesus to be more than a prophet. Only outsiders—like Pilate, Herod, and the mocking soldiers—call Jesus a king. His kingdom is not of this world.

In Jewish tradition, the priest is a designated mediator between humanity and God. The high priest offers prayers and sacrifice, interceding with God for the people. Jesus, in this sense, is thus the ultimate High Priest because, at the Last Supper, he offers himself for sacrifice and prays to the Father for his disciples. The explicit identity that Jesus claims at the Last Supper, however, is that of servant: "I am among you as one who serves" (Luke 22:27).[4] There is a risk that the identity of Jesus as High

---

2. See also Matt 16:13–23 and Luke 9:18–22.
3. See Pagola, *Jesus*, 317–50.
4. See also Matt 20:28; Mark 10:45; John 13; Phil 2:7.

Priest might dominate our images of Jesus. This can lead to clericalism, as Pope Francis has often noted, and smother the images of prophet and servant.[5]

Jesus has many identities. He fits no formula.[6] Jesus was and is the child of Mary and the Son of God. He is part of the divine mystery. You could find him in the cowboy church, or on the road, or in a hospital ward, or among those who seek to build a just society. You could find him among priests, servants, and prophets. You will find him where people gather in his name. You will certainly find him in a refugee camp. Where your world gets broken open, there, if you look, you will find him. He is with you always. That is his promise. Then you will recognize him for who he really is.

5. See, e.g., Pope Francis, Apostolic Journey to Chile and Peru, "Meeting with the Bishops," Santiago Cathedral Sacristy, January 16, 2018.

6. See Eduard Schweizer, "Jesus: The Man Who Fits No Formula," in *Jesus*, trans. David E. Green (Richmond, VA: John Knox Press, 1971), 13–51.

11

WHY DID JESUS HAVE TO DIE SUCH A HORRIBLE DEATH?

This is a caring and reasonable question. To outsiders, from the time of St. Paul, this Christian belief in a crucified God was ridiculous, even scandalous. Surely a loving God who allows such a death can only really be callous and coldhearted. But Jesus didn't *have* to die like this. He *chose* to die. His death was a profound act of infinite self-giving love.

Have no doubt. Jesus died on a cross. His heart was pierced, and he breathed a last breath. The Gospels relate, at some length, the same story of how, where, and when Jesus was crucified. The Roman historian Josephus reports that crucifixions were common at this time, and Philo of Alexandra is scathing about Pontius Pilate, who was known for "frequent executions without trial, and endless, horrible cruelty."[1]

The Gospels are clear that Jesus *chose* to go to Jerusalem, all the while knowing that he would be arrested and killed: "When the days drew near for him to be taken up, he set his face to go to Jerusalem" (Luke 9:51).[2] He did not go submissively to his death. He embraced death. But why couldn't God have saved him? Here are four responses.

First, Jesus had to die simply because he was human, and dying is part of human life. Death is part of life, and life is part of death. No matter how long we think we can live in space and time, entropy will slowly wind us down. If Jesus had not shared in death, then he would not have been fully sharing in human life. He would have been a fair-weather friend, a fraud. He would not have been in solidarity with us. He would

---

1. See Pagola, *Jesus*, 362, 370.
2. Note that the expression "to be taken up" means "taken up into heaven" and refers to Jesus's crucifixion and resurrection.

have quit when the going got tough. But Jesus stayed the course. His death settled any doubts about his humanity once and for all. He faced death with the same fear and dread as any other human being. He endured as terrible a death as one could imagine. He is in complete solidarity with us, especially with those who innocently suffer a cruel death. He will show us that death is not the end of life. He is human, and where he goes, we can go too. Instead of clinging to mortal life, which must end, we are set free to fall upward into the hands of God. That was how Jesus died. He sets a model for how we can die.

Second, if God had saved Jesus from death, then Jesus's teaching would be hollow. The core of Jesus's teaching is that we give ourselves to our neighbor, that we think less about our own life and more about the lives of others, and that we love God with all our heart and all our strength, even beyond our capacity for understanding. Jesus asks us to give everything, even unto death. Jesus reveals a divine love in choosing to face death. He trusts in eternal love even when he feels this human suffering is beyond him, even when he feels forsaken by God. He gives himself to both the will of the authorities and the will of the Divine. His death is as lonely as any human death. The seed must be buried in the ground to bring forth new life.

In the earliest Christian memory, death was central to the way of Jesus.[3] Jesus tells his disciples, "Whoever does not carry the cross and follow me cannot be my disciple" (Luke 14:27; see also Matt 10:38; Mark 8:34). This carrying of the cross consists of little steps and big steps: we die to being self-centered; we die to the superficial pressures of our society; we grow spiritually; and, in the end, we are prepared to die once and for all and to enter eternity. This is a way of radical conversion.

Third, and this is an elaboration of the previous two points, if God had saved Jesus from death, there would still be a gap between us and God. We would still have to face the inevitability of evil, violence, diminishment, and death, the constancy of frustrated hope. Nothing we could do would close that gap. The reality of suffering, injustice, and evil in the world needs to be addressed, Ratzinger argues, because it "disfigures the world and distorts God." He then turns the question about God causing suffering on its head. In Jesus's death, instead of God demanding sacrifice to ward off suffering, God embraces the whole of the worst of human experience and drinks the dregs of the cup of suffering in an act of infinite love.[4] Light overcomes darkness. There is now a possibility that our lives can be lived in a new context: not meaningless, not despairing, not weighed down by a sense of sin, but hope filled. Nothing, no

---

3. See Borg, *Meeting Jesus Again for the First Time*, 86, 94–95.
4. Joseph Ratzinger/Pope Benedict XVI, *Jesus of Nazareth*, 232.

matter how terrible, can now separate us from the love of God: "For God so loved the world that he gave his only Son, so that everyone who believes in him may not perish but may have eternal life" (John 3:16). The death of Jesus is not a sacrifice so much as a revelation; it is the infinite love of God, not the callousness of God.

Fourth, and following from the above, if Jesus did not die, then there could be no experience of his resurrection, no sense of what the fullness of human life entails. While Jesus was not saved from death, that was not the end of the story. The power of divine love is shown both in allowing Jesus to choose death and in raising Jesus up. The death and resurrection of Jesus show us that death is not the end of life. Jesus embraced the ultimate diminishment of death and revealed a risen life. Death does not conquer him. He conquers death. Where he goes, we can follow.

12

WAS THE TOMB EMPTY?

Where did Jesus go after the crucifixion? The Gospels tell us that Jesus was placed in a tomb after his death, and that two days later, the tomb was found to be empty. Nobody witnessed the actual resurrection. All they found was an empty tomb. Was the tomb really empty?

What normally happened after a man was crucified? The Romans left his body to hang on the cross as a public warning, eventually to be consumed by vultures and wild dogs. Any remains after that were thrown onto a common grave. For the Jews, however, a corpse had to be buried on the day of death. Given both the importance of ritual cleanliness and the imminence of the solemn Feast of the Passover, it is plausible that Jesus was taken down from the cross and buried on the eve of the Sabbath.[1] All the Gospels agree that this is what happened. His body was taken by Joseph of Arimathea, wrapped in linen and spices, and laid in a tomb that had just been hewn out of the rocks. A stone was then rolled across the front of the tomb (see Matt 27:57–60; Mark 15:43–46; Luke 23:50–55; John 19:38–42). One biblical scholar speculated that Jesus's body was laid in a shallow grave and then carried away by wild dogs, but his suggestions have been rejected as "almost entirely wrong" and "unsalvageable."[2]

According to the Gospels, early in the morning on the day after the Sabbath, some disciples came to the tomb to tend to Jesus's body. They did not anticipate anything like resurrection, but they found the stone rolled away and the tomb empty. Such consistency across all four Gospels is rare. Could this be a true story or has it been manufactured? Either Jesus's body was secretly taken away and the story of the resurrection was manufactured, or something extraordinary happened.

---

1. See Deut 21:22–23; Ratzinger, *Jesus of Nazareth: Holy Week*, 224; Pagola, *Jesus*, 403–4.
2. John Dominic Crossan proposed this rationale for the disappearance of Jesus's body. The critical comments come from N. T. Wright, *Jesus and the Victory of God* (Minneapolis: Fortress, 1996), 44, and a review of Crossan, *The Historical Jesus*, by Ben F. Meyer, *The Catholic Biblical Quarterly* 55, no. 3 (1993): 575–76.

If the story of the empty tomb was manufactured, why in such a patriarchal era would the key witnesses be grieving women? If the point of the manufactured story is to prove the resurrection of Jesus, why wouldn't a witness of the resurrection itself be produced? The only physical evidence is the empty tomb. There are no witnesses; there are no details. All we know is that when they were permitted to visit the tomb, on the day after the Sabbath, Jesus's body was missing. It implies that something happened to Jesus's physical remains.

There is a telling silence in both the Gospels and the Creeds about what exactly happened at the resurrection. Note, also, that the word *body* had a different meaning in Jesus's time. It did not just mean our physical body as a collection of muscle and bone. It meant our recognizable person, with all its scars and idiosyncrasies, so that our body represents our person and our life story. (See more in "A Scientific Postscript" below.)

The Gospels, however, do offer several accounts of what happened after the discovery of the empty tomb. Jesus's followers are devastated, disheartened, and afraid. Jesus appears to Mary Magdalene as she weeps outside the tomb, but she thinks he is the gardener. How could this be? He then appears amid the disciples in Jerusalem, even though the door is locked. How did he do that? He walks unrecognized beside the two disciples on the road to Emmaus. How could that happen? Jesus waits unrecognized on the shore of the Sea of Galilee, which is a long way from Jerusalem, when Peter and his friends are fishing. What is that about?

These are astonishing stories, quite different from the stories about Jesus before his crucifixion. There is a vagueness here about his appearance and movements. There seems to be a transgression of the laws of space and time. The Gospels are at least clear that Jesus didn't disappear from the scene. He reemerged into the disciples' lives, but he was different.

St. Paul talks more about the resurrection than the empty tomb. He passes on a teaching of the very first Christian communities, perhaps what he had been taught when he was being prepared for his baptism in Damascus:

> For I handed on to you as of first importance what I in turn had received: that Christ died for our sins in accordance with the scriptures, and that he was buried, and that he was raised on the third day in accordance with the scriptures, and that he appeared to Cephas, then to the twelve. Then he appeared to more than five hundred brothers and sisters at one time, most of whom are still alive, though some have died. Then he appeared to James,

then to all the apostles. Last of all, as to one untimely born, he appeared also to me. (1 Cor 15:3–8)

The Apostles' Creed and the Nicene Creed also say nothing about the empty tomb. They simply declare that Jesus was buried and on the third day rose again from the dead and ascended into heaven.

Clearly, resurrection is not a matter of coming back to life and carrying on as you were before your death. Resurrection is not the resuscitation of a corpse. Jesus is not being returned to the life he had before his crucifixion, so that he might die again another day. For the early Christians, resurrection meant a new kind of living presence. Referring to St. Paul and the Acts of the Apostles, Pagola argues that, within five or ten years of Jesus's crucifixion, the Christian community had developed a summary of their faith, and the heart of their confession was that "God has raised Jesus from among the dead." The resurrection is God's work, and it includes Jesus being raised up and exalted.[3]

So, was the tomb empty? I think so. How can I explain it being empty? Either someone stole Jesus's body, or another great act of God occurred. I choose the latter, because others have witnessed to this faith, and it is a more wonderful, beautiful, loving view of life than the narrow and unenchanted horizon of a strict materialism. Hope is better than theft.

A SCIENTIFIC POSTSCRIPT

The skeptical or scientifically minded student is entitled to ask how we can believe such a story. How can someone who is dead and buried come back to life? It might help to clarify what Christians mean by "body" and by "resurrection of the body."

Scientifically, our body is a unique collection of well-organized chemical cells made of atoms and molecules. While our DNA remains much the same, experiments using radioactive isotopes indicate that the cells in our bodies replace themselves every seven to ten years. That's why we must eat. When Christians talk about the resurrection of the body, however, they have more than a chemical body in mind. They are not thinking of the body as an inanimate object.

---

3. See Pagola, *Jesus*, 388–89.

The early Christian community, as declared in their Creeds, believed explicitly in the resurrection *of the body*. Jesus's resurrection was not just the survival of a soul, nor a spirit, nor of a ghost. By body, the early Christians meant the total person—a "subject" rather than an "object," an "I" rather than an "it." When talking about resurrection, Christians are using an existential view of the human body. Existentially, our body is what makes us unique. It is through our body that we experience warmth, hunger, intimacy, and exhaustion. Our body is how we get recognized. Our body carries our scars and the marks of our labors. Through our bodies, we love and laugh. It is through our bodies that we relate to the rest of the world, the space and time in which we live and move. Our body simultaneously limits us in space and time and pushes us to transcend these limits.

In believing in the resurrection of the body, we do not believe that Jesus's atoms and molecules were all put back together again in their original working order. That would only be resuscitation. We believe that Jesus has a body in the sense that he is still the same loving Jesus, still carries scars, is still unique, is still alive, as in a body. This risen body is different, however, in that it is not limited in space and time.

The skeptical student might rightly ask how we can be sure that there is such a thing as a risen body with these properties. We can't be sure, we can say, but we do know that physical reality is much more subtle than a collection of particles moving in space and time. We know that space and time are not absolute, but rather evolving as the universe evolves. We do not know what a risen body is like, because we haven't died yet, but it is possible that there is a deeper level of reality, an underlying reality that unites rather than separates. Physicists know about what Einstein called "spooky action at a distance" in quantum theory, and the implications of Bell's theorem for what is now called quantum entanglement, in which apparently separated realms of reality are always connected and behave as one.

We must also admit that our hopes rest on the faith and witness of the first disciples, and that taking this step of faith is a great challenge; but we can still say that this faith is not unreasonable.

13

SO WHERE IS JESUS NOW?

A pressing question! The best answer is that "Jesus is here, with us, with you." "Here" does not refer to a GPS latitude and longitude, but to a personal space: wherever we happen to be. The wording of the question is instructive. The word *where* is the clue in this question, in that, *where* only has meaning when we are in a three-dimensional, space-time framework. It only applies to specific material objects. It's easy to explain "Where is the dog?" or "Where is Australia?" It's much harder to explain "Where is love?" or "Where is the infinite?" or "Where is a voice?"

A few days or weeks after the resurrection, Scripture tells us, Jesus was lifted up into heaven. This is called the ascension. There are four things to note about the biblical accounts of Jesus's ascension. First, the ascension story continues the resurrection story. Ascension is not so much about going to some distant idyllic place called heaven, but about the perfection of a relationship with God. This is particularly evident in John's Gospel, when the risen Jesus declares, "I am ascending to my Father and your Father, to my God and your God" (John 20:17). Second, the ascension was not some force of nature, but God's work: Jesus was *taken up* into heaven. Third, the reports of the ascension are vague and inconsistent. Neither Matthew nor John explicitly mentions an ascension. Mark simply says that Jesus was taken up into heaven. And Luke, rather ambiguously, says that Jesus "withdrew from them and was carried up into heaven" (Luke 24:51, see also Mark 16:19). Fourth, because of the ascension, Jesus is seen as not only in complete union with God but also, as Matthew insists, with us to the ends of the earth and until the end of time—that is, into eternity.

In the previous chapter, we noted Mary Magdalene's confusion at meeting the risen Lord outside the empty tomb. She recognizes Jesus by his voice, not his looks! The text suggests that Mary Magdalene then reaches toward Jesus, because he says to her, "Do not hold on to me, because I have not yet ascended to the Father" (John

20:11–17). She cannot hold him as she did in the past. Jesus's body is the same and yet different. Scripture scholar Brendan Byrne explains the ascension thus:

> When Jesus has returned to the Father, a new mode of presence, transcending the limits of space and time, will be established. Until that is the case, Mary must not hinder the process by seeking to reinstate the old relationship. She must let him go to the Father so that the promised new way of being present may come about. This new presence will make available to subsequent generations, who unlike her have not walked with and touched Jesus in his prepassion life, an intimacy and a union equal to and indeed transcending that enjoyed by the original disciples.[1]

A theological understanding of "ascension into heaven" is not concerned with the scientific possibilities of travel in space and time. Heaven is not another physical location, like a distant planet. It is more a state of being. While space and time and matter separate us, love unites us. Where there is complete union, time stands still and there is no space. Theologically, the ascension is much more about Jesus being in complete union with God, where complete union necessarily transcends the limitation and divisiveness of space and time.

Letting Jesus "go to the Father" may mean something like an ascension into heaven, but that does not mean Jesus is absent. He is in union with both the divine and the cosmos. That is where Jesus is now. Philosophically, an infinite God cannot be excluded from the cosmos, because such a God would be limited and, therefore, would not be infinite. Theologically, Jesus Christ has been from the beginning in a close relationship with the whole of creation.

Creation, incarnation, and resurrection are key moments in Christ being intimately part of the universe. Christ the Word of God is with us in a universal way from the very beginning of time. The universe "unfolds in God." In Pope Francis's encyclical letter *Laudato Si'*, On Care for Our Common Home, we read,

> In the Christian understanding of the world, the destiny of all creation is bound up with the mystery of Christ, present from the beginning: "All things have been created though him and for him" (Col 1:16). The prologue of the Gospel of John (1:1–18) reveals Christ's creative work as the Divine Word (*Logos*). But then, unexpectedly, the prologue goes on to say that this

---

1. Brendan Byrne, *Life Abounding: A Reading of John's Gospel* (Collegeville, MN: Liturgical Press, 2014), 333.

same Word "became flesh" (Jn 1:14). One Person of the Trinity entered into the created cosmos, throwing in his lot with it, even to the cross. From the beginning of the world, but particularly through the incarnation, the mystery of Christ is at work in a hidden manner in the natural world as a whole, without thereby impinging on its autonomy....The universe unfolds in God, who fills it completely.[2]

This idea of Jesus being at work in the natural world from the beginning, and of the divine filling the whole universe, is sometimes called the theology of the Cosmic Christ. Its origins are found in the Gospel of John and the letters of St. Paul, then in the writings of early Church figures like St. Irenaeus and St. Athanasius, and medieval scholars like St. Hildegard and St. Bonaventure, and in many twentieth- and twenty-first-century theologians.[3] The idea of the Cosmic Christ—what Byrne calls "the mystery of Christ...at work in a hidden manner in the natural world as a whole"—entails that Jesus Christ himself is always present in creation.

There is a risk in this theology of the Cosmic Christ, if misunderstood, that Jesus our brother and friend could be abandoned to a kind of nature worship. This would sell short the depths of God's love. Many peoples and cultures have found traces of the divine in nature. As such, it could be said that they have a deep sense of the Cosmic Christ even before they have heard the name of Jesus. This theology is not meant to exploit ancient beliefs but, rather, respect them. It implies that we can learn much about the Cosmic Christ through these ancient natural spiritualities, because the Word of God has always been at work in creation.[4] While ancient cultures have insights into, and words for, the holy mystery of nature, for Christians this holy mystery has a face and a name and a particular history. While Jesus Christ is always in nature, Jesus is also more than nature.

So where is Jesus now? The answer is that Jesus Christ is always with us: he is present in the immense beauty and struggle of creation; present where there is love; present in the Scriptures; present in the gatherings and sacraments of Christians; and especially present among the poor, the imprisoned, the sick, and the hungry. Perhaps this may be why Matthew ends his Gospel with Jesus saying, "I am with you always, to the end of the age."

---

2. Pope Francis, *Laudato Si'*, §§99, 233.
3. For example, Pierre Teilhard de Chardin, Elizabeth Johnson, and Denis Edwards.
4. For example, in the Australian context and reflecting on the worldview of the *Arrente* people, see Michael J. Bowden, *Unbreakable Rock: Exploring the Mystery of Altyerre* (Melbourne: Alella, 2020).

So, Jesus is right here, as close as I am to myself. The universe is not only an expression of Jesus's creative love but also a "performance art," in which the artist is fully present. Jesus Christ is the secret at the center of our world. The risen Lord invites us into the divine mystery at the heart of our almost infinite universe.

A SCIENTIFIC POSTSCRIPT

It is estimated that the distance from the Earth to the edge of the universe is about 46.5 billion light years. So, with my theological tongue stuck firmly in my theological cheek, I could say that, if Jesus were ascending into heaven from the Earth as fast as possible—namely, almost at the speed of light—and if heaven were somewhere "outside" the universe—though, according to Einstein, there is no "outside" the universe—then Jesus still has about 46 billion years to travel before he can get to heaven. Furthermore, according to Einstein's theory of relativity, if a body could travel at the speed of light, then its mass would become infinite. Perhaps the risen luminous Lord has become the almost infinite universe. Perhaps there is some super science we do not yet know about, or perhaps the word *ascension* acknowledges that we know very little about what happened.

14

HOW CAN JESUS REALLY BE IN THE EUCHARIST?

A bright young girl, sometimes called Eileen, shortly after making her first holy communion, was having a holiday with her grandparents and went with them to their Sunday Mass at our church. Her grandmother escorted her to receive the Eucharist. She nodded to the priest, who, on previous occasions, had given Eileen a blessing, to indicate that her granddaughter was now able to receive holy communion. The young girl reverently received the consecrated bread and then, being an independent spirit, went on to receive communion from the chalice—something she had not done before. She later explained that she knew that, being a child, she was not allowed to drink wine but understood that this was not wine but a sharing in the blood of Jesus. She then added with a frown, "Or was it?" I said, "It is. Things can be much more than they appear to be."

Welcome to the world of sacramental theology! At the outset, let me say that I am one of those people who genuflects toward the tabernacle and bows before receiving communion. I do this to remind myself that I am not the center of the universe and that I am just a loved speck in the presence of the infinite and holy. I believe that Jesus is wholly present in the Eucharist. This is part of my prayer and my faith. Providing a helpful explanation of the Church's teaching, however, is much more complicated. The discussion below consists of two parts: the first part is, I hope, accessible; the second part is an exploration of the Church's teaching on transubstantiation. This is more technical and difficult, and I am not sure I understand it myself!

First, we believe that Jesus is present in the Eucharist because this teaching has been handed down to us as central to our faith. In Luke's Gospel we read,

[Jesus] took a loaf of bread, and when he had given thanks, he broke it and gave it to them, saying, "This is my body, which is given for you. Do this in remembrance of me." And he did the same with the cup after supper, saying, "This cup that is poured out for you is the new covenant in my blood." (Luke 22:19–20)

Further, the Letters of St. Paul and Acts of the Apostles attest to a regular celebration of the Eucharist in the early Church and a reverence for the presence of Christ. St. Paul, writing around twenty years after the death of Jesus, reminds the Corinthians of the tradition he has received:

The Lord Jesus on the night when he was betrayed took a loaf of bread, and when he had given thanks, he broke it and said, "This is my body that is for you. Do this in remembrance of me." In the same way he took the cup also, after supper, saying, "This cup is the new covenant in my blood. Do this, as often as you drink it, in remembrance of me."...Whoever, therefore, eats the bread or drinks the cup of the Lord in an unworthy manner will be answerable for the body and blood of the Lord. (1 Cor 11:23–27)

So, from the very beginning of the Christian faith, the Eucharist is the place where we encounter Jesus Christ as fully present. But how can this be? How can we explain this to a young person? Let me begin with an analogy that I call the volcano theory of sacraments. It goes like this. When did you last think about the fact that, not far below your feet, there are rivers of molten rock that stretch all around the earth? Probably never! But if you were in Yellowstone National Park and saw boiling hot water shooting out of Old Faithful, you might start asking questions. You might find out that just three or four miles below your feet there is a twelve-mile-deep reservoir of molten rock. If you were in Bali and a volcano started shooting out smoke and ash, it would certainly grab your attention—and probably spoil your holiday. And if you came across red hot lava rolling down the mountainside of Kilauea, as often happens in Hawaii, you would be awestruck, totally attentive. My point is that *the molten rock is always there, but usually we are too preoccupied with surface issues to care about the depths.* When we see the physical presence of lava, the actual glowing streaming molten rock, we see the full reality at the heart of our planet. When the molten rock is fully present, it draws maximum attention to itself. So it is with the sacrament of the Eucharist.

Sometimes we have a religious experience or a supernatural moment when we get a glimpse of the wonder of life and the mystique of nature. This is like seeing Old

Faithful. We get an inkling of holy mystery that surrounds us. The Eucharist, however, is much more than an inkling or a glimpse. It is more like golden molten lava. In the Eucharist, the presence of the risen Lord is visible, tangible, and consumable. The faithful gather with intent, the priest puts on robes, there may be moving music and dramatic ritual. Our attention is sharply focused. Christ is declared to be, and recognized as being, present.

So, according to the volcano theory of sacraments, the risen Lord is always present among us, just as molten rock is always present beneath us, but Jesus is made noticeably present in the Eucharist, just as molten lava flowing down the side of a volcano makes the molten rock present. In other words, at the consecration, the risen Lord does not come into the bread and wine from somewhere else. Rather, at the consecration, we recognize that the risen Lord is physically present. Like disciples after the resurrection, we say, "It is the Lord!"

But how are the bread and wine the body and blood of the whole Christ? Holy communion is not a cannibalism of tissue and bone. When Jesus said, "This is my body," he was not talking about the human body as a bag of bones, but about a personal closeness, about holding and healing, breathing and bleeding, hungering and thirsting. He was talking about the locus of divine incarnation, intimacy, suffering, and nourishment. When Jesus says, "This is my blood," he is not talking about molecules of hemoglobin, $C_{2952}H_{4664}O_{832}N_{812}S_8Fe_4$. He is talking about the blood of life, about pulse and passion, about Passover, about self-sacrificing love and transformation. This is not a second-rate bodily presence. It is a complete personal presence. Dorothy Day, who spent her days between attending Mass and living with the poor, has a moving passage on the existential presence of the risen Lord in the Eucharist:

> We cannot love God unless we love each other, and to love we must know each other. We know Him in the breaking of bread, and we know each other in the breaking of bread, and we are not alone anymore. Heaven is a banquet and life is a banquet, too, even with a crust, where there is companionship. We have all known the long loneliness and we have learned that the only solution is love and that love comes with community.[1]

Now, we move from an existential faith in the Eucharist to the more difficult discussion of the Church's teaching on substantial presence. Christians held Jesus's presence in the Eucharist as an unquestioned truth for a thousand years. They did not seek to

---

1. Dorothy Day, *The Long Loneliness* (New York: Harper & Row, 1952), 286.

explain how Christ could really be present. They did not ask why the body and blood of Christ were separated out. They lived in a more open universe in which material and spiritual realities were intertwined. They celebrated the Eucharist as an intimate experience of the real presence of the risen Lord among them. This presence was part of their personal closeness to Jesus rather than a belief to be explained in words.

Starting in the Middle Ages, however, more questions were being asked about the faith. To explain how the consecrated bread and wine becomes the body and blood of Christ, St. Thomas Aquinas turned to the philosopher Aristotle for ideas about reality and change. According to Aristotle, a thing was always a combination of substance (the underlying reality that makes it what it is) and accidents (the appearances that can change while the substance remains the same). For example, my appearance can change considerably over the years, but I remain the same person. My substance remains the same, but my accidents can change.

The medieval scholars had no knowledge of modern physics. The Aristotelian theory of substance and accidents became a widely accepted view of reality. If accidents can change while substance remains the same, then substance could change while accidents remain the same. In this eucharistic theology, because substance and accidents are separable, it is possible for God to change the substance while the accidents of bread and wine remain the same. In other words, while the bread might look and taste like bread, it could become the body of Christ if the substance had been changed.

This theology of transubstantiation became central to the Church's teaching on the real presence of Christ in the bread and wine of the Eucharist at the Fourth Lateran Council in 1215 and later, more formally, at the second session of the Council of Trent (1551–52).[2] The *Catechism* acknowledges the many modes of Jesus Christ's presence among us while at the same time giving the Eucharist a special status:

> Christ Jesus...is present in many ways to his Church: in his word, in his Church's prayer, "where two or three are gathered in my name," in the poor, the sick, and the imprisoned, in the sacraments of which he is the author, in the sacrifice of the Mass, and in the person of the minister. But "he is present...most *especially in the Eucharistic species.*"...In the most blessed sacrament of the Eucharist "the body and blood, together with the soul and divinity, of our Lord Jesus Christ and, therefore, *the whole Christ is truly, really, and substantially contained.*" "This presence is called 'real'—by which

---

2. This is a long and complex story, as best described in Edward Kilmartin, "The Catholic Tradition of Eucharistic Theology towards the Third Millennium," *Theological Studies* 55, no. 3 (1994): 405–57.

is not intended to exclude the other types of presence as if they could not be 'real' too, but because it is presence in the fullest sense: that is to say, it is a *substantial* presence by which Christ, God and man, makes himself wholly and entirely present."[3]

The Church currently teaches that the bread and wine of the offertory become the body and blood of Christ at the moment of the words of consecration. This fits with the theory of transubstantiation, but not with the more Eastern view of the liturgy as being a "whole" rather than a series of parts. The Western Church's philosophical approach to the presence of Christ is helpfully complemented by the Eastern Church's more mystical theology of the relationality of all things to God. In this Eastern view, things attain their *full meaning and identity*—their *real presence* if you like—when they are fully related to God. In other words, the explanation of the eucharistic presence is not that Jesus's flesh somehow occupies the bread or that Jesus's blood somehow occupies the chalice. Rather, the change is that the bread and wine become the living body and lifeblood of Christ, just as they were always intended to be and just as they always had been. This is more like my volcano analogy. It recalls the words of Pope Francis quoted in the previous chapter: "The universe unfolds in God, who fills it completely." Bread and wine are completely filled by God's being—they become the body and blood of Christ.

Edward Kilmartin argues rather convincingly that "the prevailing official Catholic eucharistic theology that has its roots in the synthesis that began to take on characteristic traits in the 12th and 13th centuries no longer does justice to this central Christian mystery." He notes that more recent Vatican documents show an openness to "possible new theological explanations as to the 'how' of the intrinsic change."[4] It may be better to discuss the "how" of intrinsic change not in terms of how the consecration makes Christ present, but in terms of how the whole liturgy draws us into the full presence of Christ. In the terms of my volcano analogy, we should consider how in the whole liturgy we are brought to the edge of the volcano. "To participate in the Eucharist is to live inside God's imagination."[5]

---

3. *Catechism of the Catholic Church*, §§1373–74, quoting Vatican II, *Sacrosanctum Concilium*, §7; the Council of Trent, "Concerning the Most Holy Sacrament of the Eucharist," chap. 1; and Paul VI, *Mysterium Fidei*, §39. Italics here are as in the *Catechism*.

4. Kilmartin, "The Catholic Tradition of Eucharistic Theology towards the Third Millennium," 405, 431.

5. William T. Cavanaugh, *Theology, Politics and the Body of Christ*, as quoted in Walter Brueggemann, *The Prophetic Imagination*, 40th Anniversary Edition (Minneapolis: Fortress Press, 2018), xxxiv.

15

IS JESUS REALLY GOD? IS GOD REALLY JESUS?

Some questions we can answer because we have clear evidence. "Is it raining?" Go outside. Hold out your hand. If it gets wet, it is probably raining. Other questions we can answer because we have what philosophers call "justified true belief." I can tell you with some confidence that there is a town in Australia called Nar Nar Goon and, even though it looks a rather unusual name, you will probably believe me because you trust me, and because you can fact check it on the internet—though beware fake news—and this would be justified true belief.

But how do we answer these questions about Jesus? Christians firmly *believe* the answer to *both* questions is yes. Jesus is true God from true God.[1] As St. Paul states, "In him the whole fullness of deity dwells bodily" (Col 2:9). How can we justify this belief? Thinking about God is not a simple matter. Our minds are limited. Our language is inadequate. Let us try to go deeper. This chapter has a high degree of difficulty and may not be for everybody!

In short, these are impossible questions to answer if we only see the world as billions of separate entities rather than as an interconnected unity. In this world, God would be one "thing" and Jesus another "thing." So, they cannot be the same thing. Consider an example that I often use with students. I get them to look at a brick wall. I then ask, "What do you see?" They all say, "Bricks," or, "A brick wall." Nobody has ever said "Mortar" or "Cement." We materialists only see all the separate things. Not one brick touches another brick. You can see where each brick starts and ends, but the mortar is a single ribbon that holds the many bricks together. We don't notice the mortar. We don't notice the underlying unity. We don't notice the traces of God in our world.

---

1. The divinity of Jesus and the nature of the Holy Trinity are discussed in chaps. 12—13 in Honner, *Does God Like Being God?*

I am not suggesting that God is like mortar and the rest of reality is like bricks. Rather, I am pointing out that we can imagine things differently. Instead of thinking about God and the universe as a two-tiered reality—with a singular God on one tier and gazillions of things in the universe separated out on the other tier—we can think about God as being at the heart of the universe. We can then imagine that the natural and the supernatural are intimately connected. God's being is to be, and everything that "is" has been brought into being in self-giving love. Everything that "is" shares in God's being, or "isness."[2]

Many people find holy mystery in the wonder and beauty of nature, something transcendent at the heart of life, something vaguely felt even if beyond reach. Many find it difficult to take a religious step, however, and believe in the existence of a personal God. This is often because God is imagined to be an old man in some supernatural place up in the sky. The atheist Richard Dawkins, for example, argues that if we are just acknowledging the mysteries of nature when we say we believe in God, then we should do away with the word *God* and just use the word *Nature* instead. Then it would be clear that only the "*supernatural* gods" are delusional.[3]

But what if our God is a *natural* God as well as a *supernatural* God? What if reality is not two-tiered? In this view, the incarnation and the resurrection *join* the realms of the natural and the supernatural, rather than *separate* them. Such theology does not reduce God to being the same as nature, which is called pantheism. Rather, it recognizes that God is *in* nature and that nature is the epiphany of God, which is called panentheism. As Elizabeth Johnson puts it, panentheism "honors the immanence or closeness of God." Following Aquinas, she argues that not only is God in all things, but all things are in God: "that 'while God is in all things,'...it can also be said that 'all things are in God.'"[4]

Contemporary science can also be seen to blur the distinction between the natural and the supernatural. Physicist and atheist Lawrence Krauss, for example, argues that science takes us "on a journey to the heart of those mysteries that lie at the edge of our understanding of space, time, and the forces that operate within them." This

---

2. Some of these questions about God's being and God's place in the universe are treated in Honner, *Does God Like Being God?*, esp. chaps. 6, 12, and 15.

3. Richard Dawkins, *The God Delusion* (London: Black Swan, 2006), 36. See also p. 41: "The metaphorical or pantheist God of the physicists is light years away from...the God of the Bible."

4. Elizabeth A. Johnson, *Ask the Beasts: Darwin and the God of Love* (London: Continuum, 2014), 147, quoting Thomas Aquinas, *Summa Theologica*, 1.8.1.

journey includes an exploration of the "transcendental mysteries" of the meaning of life so that "we are going to be surprised at every turn."[5] In other words, the natural world may not have precisely defined boundaries. There is no sharp distinction between the natural and the supernatural.

The question "Is Jesus really God?" can thus be seen to have a reversed intent. It is not asking whether Jesus is really the same as an ineffable supernatural being. It is asking whether an ineffable supernatural being could really be the same as Jesus.

Let us go deeper still. One of my favorite books, partly because of its title, is Eberhard Jüngel's *God as the Mystery of the World*. It was written during the "Death of God" debates amid an earlier epidemic of atheism. Jüngel argued that the "Death of God" conversation was about a distant God, a God who no longer has a place in our culture and language. He argued that instead of leaving God relatively remote and impersonal, a Christian must return to "what is most authentic" in Christianity, the faith that "identifies God with the crucified man Jesus."[6] On this view, Jesus reveals the face of God. As Jesus puts it, "Whoever has seen me has seen the Father" (John 14:9). God can be in the world, and God can be Jesus. The universe is all God's show and tell. We learn that the human can bear the divine, and the divine can be human.

If Jesus is God's reconciling incarnation in the world, then, in Christian faith, Jesus is unique and qualitatively different from all others. He is not another Elijah, nor is he the equivalent of a Buddha. This belief in the uniqueness of Jesus Christ is a bold claim, to some an outrageous claim. It rests on an argument that goes as follows. There are some things that can only be done once. You can only be born once. So also, God can only create this universe once. And God can completely reconcile creation and divinity only once, because when it is completed, then it is completed once and for all. This is because God's self-giving is perfect.

The completeness and uniqueness of Christ does not mean that all other religions and all other holy men and women are worthless. Quite the reverse. Because of the Word's presence in the world from the beginning, the universe is full of holy women and men who, in a sense, are Jesus's kindred spirits. Outbreaks of the Spirit in cultures and religions through all of history are to be treated with reverence as responses to the presence of God. All creation shares in Christ's uniqueness.

---

5. Lawrence M. Krauss, *The Greatest Story Ever Told...So Far* (London: Simon & Schuster, 2017), 6, 302–3.
6. From the English translation of the 3rd ed., Eberhard Jüngel, *God as the Mystery of the World* (Grand Rapids, MI: Eerdmans, 1983), ix–x.

Recall the question Jesus asked his disciples, "But who do you say that I am?" and Peter's answer, "You are the Messiah, the Son of the living God" (Matt 16:15–16). This is the certitude of faith. It is like the certitude of tested love. It rests on knowing a person and the evidence of their words and deeds. But can we explain the certitude of our faith in Jesus being God any more than that? Our minds struggle. In chapters 21 and 22 you will find further discussion of this question.

16

WHAT SHOULD I CALL JESUS?

"How should I address Jesus? What should I call him?" These are beautiful questions, asked by someone who wants to have Jesus as a friend. "What would you like to call him?" might be the first response. You could also ask, "What do you think Jesus would call you?" or "What do you like most about Jesus?"

We have formal names for Jesus, like "Our Lord Jesus Christ, only Son of God." Informally, many people today call Jesus "Dear Lord" or "Sweet Jesus" or "Lord" or "Holy Lord." Some bow their head as they say his name. I follow the example of St. Ignatius, who addressed Jesus as "Dearest Lord." St. Catherine of Siena's prayers are often addressed to "My Sweet Lord."

Curiously, Jesus is rarely addressed by name in the Gospels. His friends call him "Teacher" or "Lord." Mary Magdalene calls Jesus "Rabbouni," which is an Aramaic variation on "Rabbi," meaning "teacher" or "master." Jesus is called "Rabbi" by the disciples, by the following crowd, by Peter, by Nathaniel, by Nicodemus, and by Judas, who betrays him. The people who did call him Jesus were an unlikeable bunch: an unclean spirit who abused him, the soldiers who arrested him in the Garden of Gethsemane, and Pontius Pilate who condemned him to death (see Luke 4:34; John 18:7; Matt 27:37). Hardly Jesus's friends.

His name wasn't really Jesus. "Jesus" is the English version of a Latin word, *Jesus*, which, in turn, was used to translate the Greek spelling, *Iesous*, of the Hebrew name "Yeshua," which is itself a variation on the names Joshua and Yehoshua, which means "salvation," or "the one who saves."

His name wasn't really "Christ" either. This is the English version of the Greek word *Kristos*, which translates the Hebrew word *mashiah* or Messiah, the anointed one. "Christ" is a title rather than a surname. To say "Jesus Christ" is to say "Jesus, the anointed one of God" or "Jesus, the Messiah."

Do not worry about all these names and their translations. Jesus Christ was born for all nations and all languages, and it is proper that his name is adapted as his story spreads across cultures. He knows what we mean. Jesus is not one to stand on his dignity and demand that we bow and scrape or call him by the right name. At the same time, as we begin to relate to Jesus, we cannot help but feel tenderness, admiration, and reverence. The words we speak to him will be both respectful and personal. St. Paul, who was overwhelmed by Jesus, thus wrote "at the name of Jesus every knee should bend, in heaven and on earth and under the earth" (Phil 2:10). While our relationship with Jesus may remain reverent, it will gradually become intimate and undying. I say "Oh Lord" a lot!

Coming to know Jesus is a lifelong pleasure. In the end, the names do not matter too much. We become closer than that, and words are entirely unnecessary.

17

DID JESUS START THE CHURCH?

Yes, Jesus did start the Church, though in a roundabout way. He probably did not quite envisage the Church as we know it today. Pope Francis is very vocal about the need for the Church to return to "the freshness of the origins."[1] But what do those "beginnings" look like? In the early days of the Church, we read,

> All who believed were together and had all things in common; they would sell their possessions and goods and distribute the proceeds to all, as any had need. Day by day, as they spent much time together in the temple, they broke bread at home and ate their food with glad and generous hearts, praising God and having the goodwill of all the people. (Acts 2:44–47)

The first time the word *church* is specifically used in the Acts of the Apostles, however, occurs after an incident which would be described as corruption today. A man sells a piece of property but does not share all the proceeds with the community. He and his wife suddenly die, and a great fear seizes the "the whole church" (Acts 5:11). Perhaps the Church in the beginning had some of the same problems we have today.

The Greek word we translate as "Church" is *ekklesia*. The word *ekklesia* literally means "the called-out ones," but, in the Greek at the time of Christ, it meant something like "the gathering of the community" or "the assembly." It is used over a hundred times in the Acts of the Apostles and the letters of St. Paul. It is no surprise, then, that *ekklesia* became the common name adopted by the Greek-speaking early Christian communities.

The word *ekklesia* only appears twice in the Gospels, both times near the end of the Gospel of Matthew (see Matt 16:18; 18:17). Some might argue, therefore, that Matthew's Gospel is stretching a point and that Jesus had no intention of founding

---

1. Pope Francis, Profession of Faith with the Bishops of the Italian Episcopal Conference, May 23, 2013, https://www.vatican.va/content/francesco/en/homilies/2013/documents/papa-francesco_20130523_omelia-professio-fidei-cei.html.

a Church. It could then be argued that the Church is an aberration of Jesus's message. Some have said that Jesus preached the kingdom of God, but all we got was the Church of Rome.

I do not share this view. To begin with, we should not just focus on the specific word *ekklesia* so much as on the gathering of the faithful. Jesus spoke in Aramaic and would not have directly used the word *ekklesia*, but he called people to follow him some twenty-three times. He was creating what might be called a social movement today.

Christianity was never meant to be a private affair. Jesus gave his followers a mission to spread the good news of God's love, to heal the sick, and to forgive sins. He promised to be with them wherever they *gathered* in his name. He wanted his disciples to continue his mission. This certainly looks like what we might call an *ekklesia*. A good definition of the Church is "the continuation of the mission of Jesus in the world."

According to the Acts of the Apostles, and the Church's teaching, the Church began after Jesus's ascension, because it was at Pentecost that the Holy Spirit descended on the apostles. It could be argued, then, that Jesus did not start the Church, but some nuance is needed here. Scripture and Tradition both recognize that the Church is born out of Jesus's self-giving love and his gift of the Holy Spirit.[2] So, even if indirectly, Jesus does start the Church.

There is much more to say about the Church, of course, but these will be matters for a third book in this series, on tricky questions about the Church.

---

2. See *Catechism of the Catholic Church*, §§766–71.

18

IF JESUS IS THE ANSWER, WHAT IS THE QUESTION?

An elderly aunt, who had great faith in Jesus and little time for theologians, used to call me smarty-pants and worse. She would have called this question a smarty-pants question, but it is a question worth pondering. Questions are important in the Gospels. Maybe Jesus is not an answer so much as a question.[1]

This question probably arose as a teenager's reaction to the WWJD ("What would Jesus do?") movement. This is a good question to ask, but perhaps Jesus is not the answer to every question. There are some questions we must answer for ourselves. Following Jesus means more than doing what Jesus would do. Following Jesus means knowing Jesus's enduring love for me as a unique individual. Rather than prescribing what we are to do, Jesus encourages us to be who we are meant to be. Jesus opens rather than closes doors.

Sometimes, our questions reveal more about what we know than our answers do. Try holding an examination in which the student who asks the best question gets the highest mark. John's Gospel begins with the priests and Levites asking Jesus, "Who are you?" and this is followed by Jesus asking two of John the Baptist's disciples, "What are you looking for?" (John 1:19, 38). While Jesus is asked 183 questions in the Gospels, he directly answers only four of them. On another count, Jesus himself asks a total of 397 questions in the Gospels.[2] Jesus often answers a question with a question.

When Jesus did answer questions, he certainly tested his followers. Consider the case of the rich young man. He asked Jesus, "Good Teacher, what must I do to inherit eternal life?" Jesus told him to "go, sell what you own, and give the money to

---

1. See Martin B. Copenhaver, *Jesus Is the Question* (Nashville, TN: Abingdon, 2014).
2. I thank Dr. Peter Mudge for his contributions to this data.

the poor...then come, follow me" (Mark 10:17–21). The rich young man then walked away sad. Some others asked Jesus, "What must we do to perform the works of God?" Jesus told them to believe in the one that God has sent. They couldn't do that, and they too walked away. Jesus then asked his closest companions, "Do you also wish to go away?" (John 6:28–29, 67). They stayed with him.

The important questions we have to consider about Jesus are ultimately these: "Do I believe in Jesus? Or will I also go away?" There is a time to speak and a time to be silent, and a time to move from our questioning brain to our committing heart. The crucial question is neither *what we are to do* nor *what we are to believe.* Rather, the crucial question is about *who we believe in.* It is about our relationship with Jesus.

To believe in Jesus is to believe in God's future. There are no absolute specific directions, but there are love and hope. We choose to walk with Jesus, and we know Jesus is walking with us. I like the quotation from Rebecca Solnit: "To hope is to give yourself to the future—and that commitment to the future is what makes the present inhabitable."[3] Commitment of the heart is significantly deeper than an answer from the brain. If Jesus is the answer, perhaps we should stop asking any more questions. If we are this fascinated by Jesus, let us get on with a life lived in his company, just like that elderly aunt.

---

3. Rebecca Solnit, *Hope in the Dark* (Edinburgh: Canongate, 2005).

Part Two

ADVANCED QUESTIONS

19

ARE THE GOSPELS FAKE NEWS?

Almost everything that we know about the life of Jesus comes from the Gospels of Matthew, Mark, Luke, and John. The word *Gospel* is derived from the Old English *godspel*, meaning good news or good tidings. This is a fair translation of the Greek word *evangelion*. But are the Gospels too good to be true? Or are they fake news?

In the twenty-first century, we sometimes wishfully hope the news is all true. Unfortunately, this is rarely the case. It is impossible to be completely objective, even in science, because we cannot help but see things through our own chosen frameworks.[1] Nonetheless, while there is news that may not be true in every detail, it may still contain an important core of truth.

For example, there is a wonderful story about Mahatma Gandhi and his sandal. Gandhi became the leader of nonviolent resistance to British rule in India. He had been a London-trained lawyer in a three-piece suit, but he became one of the poor. He sometimes wove the material for his own clothes, and he sometimes made his own sandals. One day, while rushing to get on a train, he slipped and one of his sandals fell on the station platform. He tried to get it back but was too late because the train was moving off. Quick as a flash, he threw his other sandal back onto the platform. "Better that one man has both sandals," he explained.

There are many versions of this story: one involves shoes; another has the sandal falling on the railway track. There are equally many versions of what Gandhi said, but every story involves a train and Gandhi throwing one piece of footwear away. There is no historical evidence to back up this story. There are no photos, no testimonies. Is the story true or was it invented? Either way—and this is the point—the story reveals a truth about Gandhi: Gandhi was other-centered. He was more concerned about the person who found a sandal than he was about having lost a sandal. The story may not

---

1. For more on the "really true," see chap. 21 below.

be true in every detail, but it contains an important core of truth. Self-giving love is possible. Good news.

Stories about Gandhi have a context. There was much reporting of Gandhi's activities, of what he wore, what he wrote, what he did, and what he said. There are photos and films and newspaper records. There are people alive in India, South Africa, and England whose grandparents knew Gandhi personally. Even so, while it should be easy to separate what has a core of truth from what seems completely fake, there are disputed views of Gandhi. For example, there is debate about whether he was once a communist. Truth is hard to find, and people have different understandings of truth.

When asking about the truth of the Gospels, we should remember that two thousand years ago people had a different view of history. Stories of the past were not so much about *what specifically happened* as about *what happened to us*; there were no films, no photos, and rarely were these stories written down. From generation to generation, different colors and details were added. But as with the Gandhi story, there would have been many Christians in the early Church whose grandparents knew about Jesus. The core truths remained the same.

Some people argue that the Gospels cannot be true because they differ in too many details. There are differing accounts of Jesus's birth, inconsistent versions of the Beatitudes and the Our Father, conflicting reports of Jesus's journeys to Jerusalem and the Last Supper, and wide variations in the accounts of the resurrection. There are many cases where events seem similar, yet the times, places, and names vary. If any one of these stories is true, the skeptics argue, then the others must logically be false.

As with the story of Gandhi's sandal, what is important for the people telling the Gospel stories is not consistency of detail so much as the coherence of the core message, even though many details may be true and widely reported events arguably happened. Memories of what Jesus said and did were passed from one community to another before they were written down. Each community would have given the story a particular flavor. We should expect differences of detail. Paradoxically, these differences point to the authenticity of the Gospels because, if they are not precisely consistent, then arguably they were not invented by a single individual and must have belonged to widespread communities. The Gospels also offer varying accounts because they are portraying a complex figure, both human and divine, and so eluding simple description. The different perspectives enrich a coherent picture of Jesus.

There is one last point to make about the four Gospels being anchored in reality. There were several versions of Gospels circulating in the early Church, but most were dismissed as "fake." The Gospels of Thomas, Judas, and Mary Magdalene, for example, appeared in sects but were not more widely accepted. They were judged to misrepresent Jesus and his message—what might be called "alternative facts"—and were called apocryphal. While "apocryphal" means "obscure" rather than "fake," the wider Christian community had a sense for what was the true good news about Jesus.

While there is little doubt that Jesus really did exist, as shown in chapter 1, what remains in dispute is the historical accuracy of the Gospels. Is everything historically true? There are three views on this question. First, there is the widely held view, based on what the scholars call historical-critical method, that the Gospels are the product of the early Church's experience of Jesus the Christ rather than a historical record of what Jesus of Nazareth said and did. On this basis, the Gospels tell us what the early Christian community came to *believe about Jesus* more than being *reports of what he actually said and did.* The Gospels are thus said to portray the "Christ of faith" rather than the "historical Jesus." Recalling our story about Gandhi's sandal, the Gospels may be said to contain a core truth rather than a historical truth.

The second view of the historical accuracy of the Gospels holds that they are based in evidence, but that the evidence arises out of a human experience of Jesus rather than an objective record of what he said and did. This evidence concerns experiences of Jesus before and after his resurrection. This continuity of experiences shapes the narrative. Marcus Borg, for example, holds that "the post-Easter Jesus is not just the product of early Christian belief and thought, but an element of *experience....*The post-Easter Jesus is real." While the Gospels are not "straightforward historical documents," they are "true stories" if "not literally true."[2] There is a difference here between the Gandhi story about the sandal and the Gospel stories about Jesus. The Gandhi story may not have happened, may never have been experienced, but nonetheless contains a core truth. The Gospel stories, however, were a part of people's actual experience, including spiritual experience.

A third view is that the Gospels offer a historically accurate portrait of Jesus. Benedict XVI, writing as Joseph Ratzinger, accepts the value of the historical-critical method in understanding the Gospels, but stresses the importance of a faith-based reading. He observes, "The New Testament writings display a many-layered struggle to come to grips with the figure of Jesus" that "exceeds the scope of the historical method."[3] Or again, "Despite the differing theological viewpoints, it is the same faith

---

2. Borg, *Meeting Jesus Again*, 10–18.
3. Ratzinger, *Jesus of Nazareth: From the Baptism in the Jordan to the Transfiguration*, xxi–xxii.

that is at work, and it is the same Lord Jesus who is encountered."[4] So, Ratzinger concludes,

> I trust the Gospels....I wanted to try to portray the Jesus of the Gospels as the real, "historical" Jesus in the strict sense of the word....I believe that this Jesus—the Jesus of the Gospels—is a historically plausible and convincing figure.[5]

The great Protestant theologian Karl Barth had similarly reacted against the view that historical rigor offered more truth than the witness of faith. He argued that the revelation found in the Bible and interpreted within the Church had its own factual status in Christian faith.

On this third view, Christians accept a Gospel story to be true because it is part of a much larger body of Scripture and Tradition which the Christian community holds to be true. This is because the focus of the Gospel is more on *the truth of salvation* than on *the truth of historical detail*. The risk here, however, is that we adopt an uncritical and fundamentalist reading of Scripture. We might read the verses but miss the core truth of the whole.

As teachers, we cannot expect young people to endure these theological distinctions. If a young person were to ask me, "Did Jesus walk on water? Yes or no?" I would answer, "Christians believe it's a yes, because Jesus will do anything he can to help us when we are in trouble, because he loves us." At this stage, the young person would usually pull a thinking and wondering face. So, I then add, "Look, the real miracle is not the walking on water, but that God is among us; and if God is among us, who knows what can happen?" The young face then gets more quizzical!

We could also explain to a young person that there are some matters that we can easily talk about, and there are others that are difficult to talk about. It is easy to talk about things we can see and touch and measure, like weather reports, or how tall someone is, or how long it takes to fly to Los Angeles. This might be true news, but it is not very interesting news. There are other things that are much more difficult to talk about: how someone feels, why someone is stunning, what makes for great art, and whether there are angels or not. This is the interesting news. The founder of quantum physics, Niels Bohr, once said something like this: "There are two kinds of truths: an ordinary truth is a statement whose opposite is a falsehood. A profound

---

4. Ratzinger, *Jesus of Nazareth: From the Entrance into Jerusalem to the Resurrection*, xiv.
5. Ratzinger, *Jesus of Nazareth: From the Baptism in the Jordan to the Transfiguration*, xxi–xxii.

truth is a statement whose opposite is also a profound truth. These are the interesting truths." So also, the Gospel truths.

Because the truths of the Gospel are profound and sometimes difficult to understand, we should let ourselves be guided by the wisdom of the faith community, as expressed in the teaching of the Church. The Second Vatican Council document on the Bible, *Dei Verbum*, is particularly helpful here:

> The books of Scripture must be acknowledged as teaching solidly, faithfully and without error that truth which God wanted to put into sacred writings for the sake of salvation....However, since God speaks in Sacred Scripture...in human fashion, the interpreter of Sacred Scripture, in order to see clearly what God wanted to communicate to us, should carefully investigate what meaning the sacred writers really intended, and what God wanted to manifest by means of their word....For truth is set forth and expressed differently in texts which are variously historical, prophetic, poetic, or of other forms of discourse....The living tradition of the whole Church must be taken into account along with the harmony which exists between elements of the faith.[6]

In summary, the truths of the Gospels are subtle rather than blunt, profound rather than simple. They are truths of history and truths of eternity.

So, are the Gospels fake news? Definitely not! As José Pagola says, the arrival of God is "the best news."[7]

---

6. Vatican II, *Dei Verbum,* Dogmatic Constitution on Divine Revelation, §§11–12.
7. Pagola, *Jesus,* 106.

20

HOW ARE WE MEANT TO READ THE GOSPELS?

If the Gospels deal with profound truths, how are we meant to read them? The short answer is that we do not read them as just another book. We read them in a spirit of hope and love and openness to God, allowing ourselves to be guided by the same Spirit that Jesus gave to the early Christian community. We travel them slowly, in the company of Jesus.

The Gospels may look like four small books about the life and times of Jesus, but they are more than histories or biographies. They reflect the memories and insights of the early Christian communities and their experiences of Jesus before and after his resurrection. Before the early communities talked about being Christian or being Church, they talked about themselves as "the Way" because they followed Jesus, who was the way.

The Gospels are to be used as guides through the journey of life. They inspire and comfort us. They put us in the company of Jesus. When we read any great works of literature, we enter into the company of the writer, and we learn a new way of seeing the world. We read Jane Austen, and we see pride and prejudice in new ways. We read Fyodor Dostoevsky, and we can face suffering with courage and renewed hope. We read J. K. Rowling, and we want to be as brave and resourceful as Harry Potter. So also, we read the Gospels, and we learn to travel with Jesus. But there is a very significant difference between Harry Potter and the Gospels. Jesus is real.

How did the early Christian communities decide on what went into the Gospels? Consider the following analogy of an art exhibition. Suppose a major art gallery is holding a retrospective exhibition of the paintings and drawings of a great artist—say Vincent van Gogh—and it aims to collect and display every van Gogh painting possible. There is no question about the authenticity of many of his works, but some seem inferior; others are viewed as forgeries. The experts make their judgments, though much debate remains. The people who love van Gogh make their judgments, though once again there are differences of opinion.

Imagine, however, if Vincent van Gogh himself were to walk through the exhibition with you, identifying both the authentic and the fake. He might point at one painting and say, "That one's mine," or, perhaps in horror, "That's not mine, it has no beauty, it's a fake." That would certainly end any differences of opinion. He would have authenticated his own work, and he would have taken your appreciation of his art to a new level.

In the case of the authenticity of the Gospels, the primary artist is not Matthew, Mark, Luke, or John. The primary artist is the Spirit of God moving in the early Christian community. This is the same Spirit that, according to the Book of Genesis, hovered over creation. This is the Spirit that came over Mary when Jesus was conceived, and the same Spirit that drove Jesus into the desert. This is the Spirit that Jesus promised he would send to guide his disciples after he had left them. And, finally, this is the Spirit present in the early Christian communities as they gathered the threads that made up the Gospels. Like van Gogh at his exhibition in the art gallery, this same Spirit guided the early Christian communities as the Gospels took shape. It guided them and confirmed them as they put the Gospels together. This same Spirit moves with the faith community today through the theatre of life, helping us see the truth about Jesus, helping us take our appreciation of the Gospels to a different level.

So, if we are meant to read the Gospels by traveling them with the Holy Spirit, how do we do this in practice? It doesn't mean taking a road trip, even though the Gospels are largely about a road trip. It means reading them as a guide for our lives. Reading the Gospel becomes a dialogue between the past and the present as we travel the road of life. Our wise elders remind us that it takes time to become friends with Jesus. We learn to place ourselves in Gospel situations and be with Jesus. After we have done that, we learn to find Jesus in our own situations.

It is wise to learn some basic details about the Gospels. There are many helpful introductions.[1] We can learn how, when, and where they were most likely written. Each of the Gospels fits a season of life, reflects a particular set of communities, feeds a particular need, and opens a new horizon. If we can come to love the Gospels for the

---

1. See, e.g., Pheme Perkins, *Reading the New Testament, 3rd Edition: Introduction* (Mahwah, NJ: Paulist Press, 2012); Margaret Nutting Ralph, *A Walk through the New Testament: An Introduction for Catholics* (Mahwah, NJ: Paulist Press, 2009); Donald Senior et al., *Invitation to the Gospels* (Mahwah, NJ: Paulist Press, 2002); Brendan Byrne, *Life Abounding: A Reading of John's Gospel* (Collegeville, MN: Liturgical Press, 2014).

way they inspire and nourish us, then we can also help young people learn to travel the Gospels and find Jesus walking with them.

The Gospel of Mark, probably the first of the Gospels to be written, is a young person's Gospel. It is written for a poor and marginalized community. There is less talk and more action. Jesus immediately moves from one situation to the next. Jesus calls for radical self-giving, even to the cross, even to hope beyond hope. Jesus is portrayed as a hidden Messiah rather than a triumphant superhero, and he is all the more real for the suffering he endures.

The Gospels of Matthew and Luke are similar to that of Mark. They each share much of the same material—a sign that there was an earlier source that was widely used across all the first Christian communities. Matthew and Luke are more reflective than Mark, however, adding more detail, more teachings, and often shaping stories about Jesus differently. They both give accounts of Jesus's birth, for example, but from different perspectives.

Luke's Gospel is for real people living ordinary lives, particularly women and children, as they seek healing, hope, and freedom. Luke's focus is on Jesus's compassion and humility, on the wonder of God being here among us in our history. Only Luke contains the unique parables of the Good Samaritan and the Prodigal Son.

Matthew's Gospel has a greater focus on religion, relating Jesus to the Jewish Scriptures as the new Moses, and setting foundations for the emerging Christian Church. Matthew's Gospel is likely to be of less interest to young people than Mark or Luke might be because it contains more teaching and less action, but it expresses an important dimension of the early Church's memories of Jesus.

Finally, there is the Gospel of John. This is a later, almost mystical, Gospel. Far more than the other Gospels, it blends the life of Jesus before his crucifixion with the life of Jesus in the early Church. It presents stories in a different way. If the character of Jesus in Mark and Luke seems all too human, the character of Jesus in John seems all too divine. As Borg states, the Gospel of John "is a powerful testimony to the reality and significance of the post-Easter Jesus, the living Christ of Christian experience."[2]

The four Gospels invite us into the life of Jesus in different ways and encourage us to find Jesus accompanying us in our own lives. In the Church, there is a long tradition of what is called *lectio divina*, which means something like "holy reading." It entails a slower, meditative reading. This can be done in many ways, as couples, communities, or individuals. I try to read the Gospel every day, usually on my smart

2. Borg, *Meeting Jesus Again*, 17.

phone, sometimes struggling through the Greek text. Sometimes my mind drifts to other parts of the Gospel. I talk with Jesus. I usually do this first thing in the morning, wondering about the problems of the day and what I need to do or say or write. Some mornings I read the Gospel while sitting on a bus when I'm heading off for a meeting and worrying about decisions that must be made. I find constant resonances between my world and the drama of the Gospels. The Gospels come alive, and I can travel with, talk with Jesus.

Young people have remarkable talent and insight if, in the right place and circumstances, they are invited to act out a Gospel scene. They have young hearts and fresh eyes. This is a form of *lectio divina.* As parents and teachers who travel with the Gospel, we can help them in their learning if we too provide a loving witness to Jesus, alive and among us. In our own way, we will be proclaiming the good news and inviting the next generation into a relationship with Jesus.

21

IS FAITH A DELUSION?

Christians have been regarded as deluded since Festus called St. Paul insane because he believed that a dead man could be raised to life (Acts 26:24). The message of the cross was seen as a joke, a folly, a nonsense (see 1 Cor 1:18–21); it was out of touch with reality.

We, too, in our secular age, encounter skepticism about, and sometimes mockery of, the Christian faith. A secular society, by definition, has its focus on a temporal and material world and is not particularly interested in dealing in the transcendent and eternal dimensions of existence. Does this mean that Christians are out of touch with reality and therefore deluded? Or are Christians, in fact, more enlightened and the secularists more myopic? The impossible may not be as nonsensical as it first appears. Perhaps reality extends beyond the material world.

Reality is hard to define. There is a view that the only reality we can be sure of is the reality that, in principle, we can see, hear, smell, touch, and taste. This is the reality of familiar day-to-day material objects. These are the things we can measure and count. This is called empirical reality and it pertains to the immanent—meaning "at hand"—world. According to this view, anything not "immanent" is unreal. The opposite of immanent is transcendent, meaning realities beyond the reach of our ordinary senses. If the immanent alone is real, then talk of transcendent realities must be delusional. Faith in transcendent realities would then be delusional.

There are two problems with a strictly empirical definition of what is real. First, there are many gray areas. For example, many of the things we consider real in physics, like gravity, neutrinos, quarks, and Wi-Fi, we cannot directly see. We can track them in scientific experiments. We see their effects and we infer they are real. Similarly, we cannot directly experience many of the things we hold as important in life, like love, truth, and art, but we consider them real.

The second problem with a strictly empirical definition of reality is that it implies a binary view of reality. In other words, it suggests that there are only two categories when it comes to talking about reality: there is the real and the unreal. In other words, it implies that we can talk about the real material world, but other talk is ultimately nonsense. It makes human beings the arbiters of reality. This assumption seems arrogant. Can a frog determine what is real in the universe? Who are we humans to judge? Great scientists, and even the new atheists, admit that there is a mystery at the heart of reality.[1]

It is true that we probably are deluded if we try to say too much about these mysteries, but that does not mean that there are no transcendent realities. The postmodernist philosophers remind us that words may trace things, but they do not match things. Like the medieval scholastic philosophers, they reject a narrow realism. Both are engaged in what is called metaphysics. In this sense, postmodernism and Christianity are friends. They both challenge a narrow understanding of reality. They are both concerned with what seems impossible: a reality that transcends the bounds of sense. This includes a God who is real, but not a God who is a material idol.[2]

When thinking about words and realities, it is important to note that all our words are pointing words. Words are not things. They point to things. They can also point to mysteries. Some words are easier to use than others. It is easier to use the word *dog* than the word *god*, but both words point to aspects of our experience and our networks of ideas. Our use of words is a work in progress, because sometimes we need to revise the meaning we give to words and the way we apply our network of ideas. For example, we still talk of sunrise and sunset, but we have revised our meanings.

Putting this another way, describing *reality* is not a simple matter, and a strictly empirical understanding of reality is narrow and inadequate. It follows that a humble exploration of realms that transcend ordinary experience is a human duty rather than a human folly. Consequently, we accept that our words about the transcendent are pointing words—or analogical—and we should be wary of assuming that our words point to an empirical reality. They point to deeper levels of reality.

---

1. See Honner, chap. 15 in *Does God Like Being God?* The militant atheist Lawrence Krauss writes eloquently about the "mystery of our existence" but humbly prefers "when addressing these transcendental mysteries...to make no assumption." See Krauss, *The Greatest Story Ever Told...So Far* (New York: Simon & Schuster, 2017), 302–3.

2. For an extraordinary study of the postmodern passion for the impossible, see John D. Caputo, *The Prayers and Tears of Jacques Derrida* (Bloomington, IN: Indiana University Press, 1997).

Rather than talk about the binary opposites of real and unreal, then, we would be wiser to talk about three possibilities: the real, the unreal, and the not yet fully known. The concerns of religion are often in this latter category. They are neither delusional nor unreal. They are reasonable, but not yet fully known. In talking about our faith, we can use pointing words like *God*, *grace*, *resurrection*, *eternity*, and *spirit*, and using them does not mean we are deluded. If we use these words humbly and wisely, we might even be enlightened.

22

CONSUBSTANTIAL....WHAT?

Our Creeds, unlike our Gospels, tell us almost nothing about the day-to-day life of Jesus. They offer no detail about what Jesus was like or what he said and did. Instead, they tell us about the significance of Jesus: he is true God from true God, one with the Father in being, through whom all things were made, and who, for us and our salvation, came down from heaven. The *Catechism* follows the pattern of the Creeds in its teachings about Jesus. What is going on here?

The Creeds established a consensus on the core contents of Christian faith and settled disputes in the early Christian communities about the nature of Jesus. Some said Jesus was a great prophet but not divine; others claimed he was divine but not truly human. The first Council of Nicaea was called in the year 325 to address the issues. Nicaea is now a small town called Iznik in modern-day Turkey, but in the fourth century it was a superbly designed metropolis at a median point between Rome, Constantinople, and Jerusalem. The Council of Nicaea involved bishops and delegates from across the Christian world. They tried to clarify and justify the Church's faith. In the Nicene Creed, they declared that Jesus was "true God from true God, begotten not made, consubstantial with the Father." You won't find the term *consubstantial* in the Gospels. The Council was trying to explain what we believed about Jesus Christ. It was doing what today we would call Christology.

The fact that the Nicene Creed says nothing specific about Jesus's day-to-day life need not close us off from following Jesus in a more personal way. The New Testament, on the one hand, presents numerous facets of Jesus that stretch our imagination and run the risk of being misunderstood. The Creeds, on the other hand, try to clarify the basic truths of Christian faith and set boundaries.

St. Paul does Christology too. He finds Jesus alive for all nations, for all creation, for all time. He reflects on how Jesus brings freedom from sin and law, how God's grace and love embraces all. He is much more explicit about Jesus being part of a divine Trinity than the Gospel writers. For Paul, Jesus is not a historical figure stuck in the past. Jesus is the face of God, here and now in our own time, the living God.

Christology should help us appreciate the continuity between the Jesus who walked the roads of Galilee two thousand years ago and the risen Lord Jesus who has existed for all time and in divine eternity before and after time. Easily said, but difficult to grasp. How can a fully human being living in history also be a fully divine being who transcends time and space? As we noted earlier, we need different perspectives to get a line on profound truths. For example, there is the perspective of Jesus's humanity, and there is the perspective of Jesus's divinity, but there is a tension between these two perspectives.

The early Creeds appealed to Greek philosophical terms like *ousios* (meaning "being" or "nature") and *hypostasis* ("underlying substance") to clarify how Jesus is both divine (the same *ousios* as God) and human (a different *hypostasis*). Distinct from the Father, and yet the same as the Father in divinity. The word "consubstantial" in the Nicene Creed is a translation of *homoousios*, meaning "of one substance."

These Greek terms may not be so helpful today. Some theologians have described the tension between Jesus's humanity and divinity in terms of doing Christology from below (the human Jesus) and Christology from above (the Divine Lord). Others have talked about the Jesus of history (living in time) and the Christ of faith (transcending time). These distinctions are helpful in approaching texts and theologies, but they ultimately run the risk of dividing Jesus. The key point in all of them, however, as Schweizer succinctly states, is that "a Jesus of Nazareth who is not seen...as the Christ of God is not Jesus of Nazareth at all."[1]

For each of us, here and now, our unique personal experience of Jesus will be appropriate and authentic. Every human being lives in limited and specific circumstances, however, and our personal experiences of Jesus will never fully define Jesus. If we focus too much on just one aspect of Jesus as a person, we might miss out on seeing the fullness of who Jesus really is. As we explore young people's questions about Jesus, and as we try to bring Jesus's life out of the past and into the present, let us draw on the manifold riches of the whole New Testament and be guided by the wisdom of the Church: that Jesus is truly divine and truly human; that Jesus is truly risen.

At this stage, we may be tempted to throw our hands up in the air and say that it is all too hard, too illogical, and too unreasonable to believe that a person can be both human and divine. It is simpler, we might say, to believe that Jesus was a really

---

1. Eduard Schweizer, *Jesus Christ: The Man from Nazareth and the Exalted Lord* (Macon, GA: Mercer University Press, 1987), 56.

good man, and a prophet of God, but not actually divine. This might be simpler, but it is not earth-shattering, and it is not our faith. While our faith in Jesus being both fully human and fully divine may stretch our imagination, it is not unreasonable. A God of infinite love is not going to hold back on self-giving. A God of infinite love would not stay at a distance but would become as intimate as possible with us. A truly and infinitely loving God would come fully among us, without pretense and without security. This is the good news.

What we have been doing in this chapter is some initial Christology. We have been trying to understand Jesus Christ better so we can both enrich and explain our faith. Christology can seem very complicated and sometimes cut across our personal relationship to Jesus, but it does serve the purpose of opening our minds and hearts to the profound heights and depths of God's love. The tricky questions about Jesus that young people ask are all christological questions, but in the end, they require cutting out the superfluous decorations and getting closer to the living Jesus.

At its core, our faith is very simple. I like the story about Karl Barth, a giant among theologians, when he first visited America. An enthusiastic reporter is said to have asked him what his latest and most important theological discoveries were. Barth is said to have replied, "Jesus loves me, this I know, for the Bible tells me so."

CONCLUSION

WHERE TO FROM HERE?

We began this book with a story about a statue called "High Five Jesus." Hopefully, in coming to the end of the book, a more vibrant Jesus has emerged: a living Jesus, a welcoming and present Jesus.

At the same time, I hope that Jesus is more than any particular image each one of us might have: he is more than a teacher, more than a healer, more than a pilgrim, more than a prophet, more than a mystic, more than a revolutionary, and certainly more than a set of teachings and doctrines. Jesus is the Word of God, present at the start of creation and present through all creation, both incarnate and transcendent, ecstatic love, who wants to call us his friends.

In an earlier book, *Does God Like Being God?*, I explained why faith is primarily personal and secondarily a set of beliefs.[1] In the Introduction to this present book, I argued that knowing Jesus precedes understanding Jesus. I referred to a point that Pope Francis made after the Synod on Youth: "Rather than being too concerned with communicating a great deal of doctrine, let us first try to awaken and consolidate the great experiences that sustain the Christian life." He goes on to say,

> Youth ministry should always include occasions for renewing and deepening our personal experience of the love of God and the living Christ. It can do this in a variety of ways....Yet this joyful experience of encounter with the Lord should never be replaced by a kind of "indoctrination."[2]

The chapters in this book, while secondary to the importance of a personal encounter with Jesus, have tried to *unfold* doctrine rather than impose it. They might be called *exdoctrination* rather than indoctrination. The aim is to help young people, who are born to ask questions, understand what it is that their parents and teachers love

---

1. See Honner, chap. 3 in *Does God Like Being God?*
2. Pope Francis, post-synodal apostolic exhortation, *Christus Vivit*, §§213–14.

and see in Jesus. While we often blame secular society for the demise of church participation, we adult members of the Church today must also look at the authenticity of our faith as well as the depths of our compassion.

Following the way of Jesus has many implications for Christian life and the practice of our faith today. This leads to many questions about the Church and about what we must hold and what we are called to change. Hopefully, it may also lead to us exploring tricky questions about the Church.

CPSIA information can be obtained
at www.ICGtesting.com
Printed in the USA
LVHW060242110622
721011LV00012B/234